THE SHABBAT CATALOGUE

by RUTH F. BRIN

Illustrated by RUTHANN ISAACSON

KTAV PUBLISHING HOUSE, INC./NEW YORK

Library of Congress Cataloging in Publication Data

Brin, Ruth Firestone.
   The Shabbat catalogue.

   1. Sabbath. 2. Family--Religious life (Judaism)
I. Title.
BM685.B66   296.7   78-11981
ISBN 0-87068-636-4

MANUFACTURED IN THE UNITED STATES OF AMERICA

To Joshua Shai Ingber

TABLE OF CONTENTS

6

8

Acknowledgments

While we cannot list all of the families whose participation meant so much to this project, we do acknowledge the help of the professional staff of the Jewish Community Center in Minneapolis, especially the Director, William Budd, the Art Director, Ruth Ann Isaacson, and the Music Director, Mordechai Shachar. Others, including Margery Sussman, Al Hersh, Barrie Segall, Aharon Shefi, Steven Rod, and Rhoda Lewin also helped. Leaders of the participating groups included Martha Birnbaum, Marge Kaplan, Mona Mortenson, Marvin Bienstock, Rae Goodman, Leonard Rosenthal, Bernard Lande, Rabbi Ludwig Nadelman, and Rabbi Sylvan Kamens.

Introduction

This book is the result of a successful experimental project called "Shabbat Shalom." Starting in the fall of 1974, more than a hundred American families began this project, which lasted almost a year and proved to be an enriching Jewish experience. Now we want to share that experience with you.

Some of the families were young couples whose children were starting a Jewish school—a nursery school, Sunday school, or Hebrew school. They wanted to enhance their home celebration of the Sabbath. Some were families who had warm memories of Shabbat at their grandparents' homes, where the grandmother baked challah and the grandfather sang the kiddush and many cousins played together. But like most American families, they found themselves living around the country, far from other relatives, so they agreed to meet in groups, at Jewish centers, synagogues, or homes, to receive material every month, and to comment on its effectiveness.

The Project was directed from the Jewish Community Center of Greater Minneapolis and financed by the Institute for Jewish Life. This book is the result of the work not only of the Writer-Coordinator and the professionals in art, music, education, and social work who helped her, but also of all the families and leaders who cooperated with their participation, evaluation, comments, questionnaires, letters, and phone calls. This is tested material. If you try our suggestions at home, we promise you a genuine and enjoyable Jewish experience.

Of one thing we are convinced: adults can't teach children to love and enjoy the Shabbat unless they themselves love it and understand it. For that reason, there are many selections that adults can read aloud at the table on Shabbat evening. Look over the other sections of this book and choose what is appropriate for your family and yourself. Be selective. Introduce only a few new things at a time, and let other members of the family select and introduce what appeals to them. Make each Shabbat different and special.

The families who helped write this book found that it enriched their lives together and deepened their feelings of Jewish identity. With thoughtful use, it will do the same for you. Shabbat Shalom!

A Few Hints on How to Begin

Try to create a special atmosphere on Shabbat—on Friday night at dinner and hopefully throughout Saturday, ending with havdalah. Many ways are suggested throughout the book, but remember:

• Try to have everyone share in some way in the preparations for the Sabbath.

• Have a meal the family enjoys, a pretty table setting, and everyone sitting down together on time.

• If your family doesn't easily assume a relaxed mood of friendship, fellowship, warmth, and happiness, invite a guest.

• If you want music, your own singing is the best. Turn off TV or radio and disconnect the phone.

• If you have very young children, remember that they like repetition, and do not expect them to intellectually understand everything. If Shabbat observance is meaningful and important to the parents, their children will "catch" their feelings. Alas, if your observance is a sterile exercise, your children will know it.

• Very young children have a short attention span. Let them leave the table Friday night and play quietly, then return for the "birkat" when you recite or sing it. In Israel and in many Orthodox synagogues here, small children wander in and out during the prayers. Our ideas of decorum are neither traditional nor applicable to little children. In other words, if your child realizes that something special happens on the Sabbath and participates in some way, this is enough. Consider your own needs and those of all the people in your family for moments of repose, happiness, contemplation, and restoration. Everyone, including the little ones, will respond.

• Choose the material in this book that best suits your family and your needs.

In order to help you find the material that is linked by similarity of theme and ideas, we have marked some of the stories, readings, crafts projects, and recipes that complement each other and can be used together.

For instance, if you wanted to have an Israeli Shabbat, you could look for the Israeli recipes, poetry from modern Israel, and an Israeli children's story and songs, all identified by this symbol.

Man rests on the Sabbath because God created the world in six days and rested on the seventh. The creation theme is identified by this symbol.

The theme of Jewish religious experience, the eternal soul of the Shabbat, is identified by our artist's interpretation of the 42nd psalm, with the prayershawl and "the service of the heart."

The Jewish family, a central theme in Jewish life, is symbolized by this open door to a Jewish home.

Everything pertaining to the havdalah service is identified by the braided candlestick.

Special customs, recipes, and stories associated with the Eastern European and Chassidic traditions can be found by looking for the Torah scrolls.

One of the greatest themes of Shabbat is the Exodus from Egypt and the giving of the Torah on Mount Sinai. Although these are celebrated at Passover and at Shavuot, they are also mentioned in the kiddush every Shabbat because these events are so central to the life of the Jewish people. Both the birth of our freedom with the ever-recurring need to champion it and the tremendous obligation inherent in our acceptance of God's words should be reconsidered and reaffirmed every week. Exodus and Sinai are symbolized by the logo of the Ten Commandments.

1

Stories for Children

Noah and the Ark:

A Story for Small Children

God made the world and everything in it. But after God made the world, he saw that men were wicked—they didn't love each other. Some of them hurt each other, and they were not kind to the animals. He decided to send a flood of water that would drown everything. Since God made the world, He also has the power to destroy it. But then He remembered Noah, who was a good man, and his wife and their three sons. The sons' names were Shem, Ham, and Japheth. God decided to save Noah and to have Noah save all the animals. So He told Noah to build an ark, a kind of wooden boat. Then He told Noah to take every kind of animal and bird on the ark, so when the flood was over, new baby animals could be born. Here's what happened:

> Noah had never made a boat
> that could float.
> His wife had never cooked a feast
> for a beast.
> Ham thought to build an ark for a bird
> was absurd.
>
> But Ham and Shem and Japheth and Noah and his
>   wife
> all worked together to save every single life.
> For forty days and forty nights
> Through growls and barks and roars and fights
> They never lost a lion or a leopard or a lark
> As they floated through the flood on the ark.
>
> When they landed on the mount
> They couldn't count

Every bird and bug and beast
they released.

Above them in the sky was a bow
God said He put it there so they would know
that He promised no more floods
to destroy each living thing,
But instead would always send
fall and winter, summer, spring,
So man and beast could grow and live,
worship God, love and give.

So you see, when we see the rainbow in the sky, we
remember God's promise to Noah, who was a good
man, and we are happy that God has made a world for
us where we can live and grow and love each other.
We are glad He has promised never to destroy all
living things again.

How Adam and Eve Learned to Build a Fire

A Jewish Legend Adapted from
Hertz, *The Jewish Prayer Book*

At the end of their first day together in the garden of Eden, Adam and Eve became very frightened. It was getting dark and cold. They began to tremble, and they thought there was something wrong with their eyes—they couldn't see well. Shadows grew around them.

Adam cried out to God for help. Now in those days, God used to walk in the garden in the cool of the evening, and he heard Adam calling.

"What is troubling you?" He asked kindly, out of the gloom.

"The sun is going away. It is getting black and cold. What will become of us?" Adam's teeth were chattering.

"I will show you what to do," God said, "but first you must find me two stones, black and hard."

Adam and Eve searched in the waning light, and they each found a stone. God looked at them.

"One of these," He said, "is called Darkness, and the other is called Shadow of Death. Now gather some twigs and dried grasses, and rub the stones together over the little pile. Have some bigger sticks ready."

While Eve finished gathering the twigs, Adam began to rub the stones together. Soon a spark flew from the stones and lit the fire. Then God showed them how to feed it with larger branches until they had warmth and light.

19

Adam was filled with joy and he exclaimed, "Blessed art Thou, O Lord our God, who creates light!" These are the very same words we say at havdalah.

But Eve, who was always curious, asked, "Why do the stones have such strange names—Darkness and Shadow of Death?"

"Because you are made in My image," came the answer, "from black, cold stones you can create bright, hot fire. You can overcome darkness, and even death, and create from them light and warmth and spiritual good."

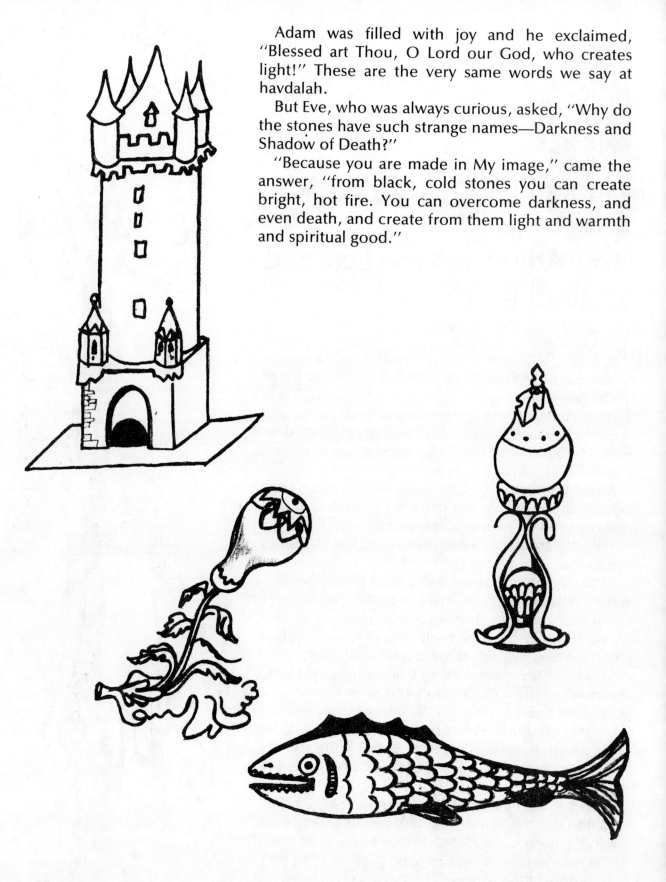

Hannele and Her Sabbath Dress

by Itzhak Schweiger

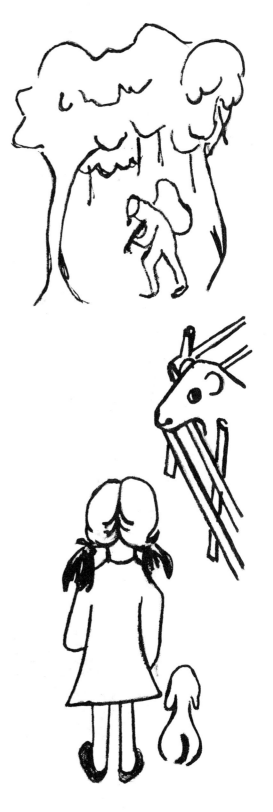

Once upon a time, in Israel, there was a little girl named Hannah. Her mother and father always called her "Hannele." Her mother worked all week to make her a beautiful white dress to wear on Shabbat. It had ruffles around the skirt. Hannele watched her mother sew and could hardly wait until she could wear the pretty dress.

Finally, one Friday, just before sunset, she washed carefully and put on the brand-new dress. She looked in the mirror, and it was very pretty! Mother said she could go outdoors until time for Shabbat dinner.

She walked slowly on the grass, not wanting to get the dress dirty. Pretty soon her little dog, Zuzie, came trotting along. Ordinarily she loved Zuzie to jump up so she could pet him, but today she said, "Down, Zuzie," very softly so he couldn't get pawmarks on her dress. "My Mommy sewed me a new dress," she told her dog, "and I don't want to get it dirty."

He trotted along behind her and they met their cow, Buttercup, who always licked Hannele's face. But Hannele moved away, "Not today, Buttercup," she said. "My Mama sewed me a new dress for Shabbat and I don't want to get it dirty."

As she walked along, Hannele saw an old man coming from the woods. He carried a heavy load, and then he sat down to rest by the path. She saw that he was very tired and old, that drops of sweat were falling from his forehead.

"Come here, little girl," he called to her.

"Shalom," said Hannele, "are you very tired?"

"Yes," he answered, "it's a very heavy load."

"What's in it?" she asked him.

"Charcoal," he explained. "What's your name?"

"Hannele." She didn't say anything for a minute, standing before him.

She saw that he was looking at her dress. "You see my dress? It's new. My Mommy made it for me for Shabbat."

"Yes, it's very pretty. Enjoy it, and wear it in good health."

"Thank you."

The old man got up and pulled the load up on his back. Hannele saw how hard it was for him. "Shall I help you?" she asked.

"Oh, thank you, yes," he answered. She walked behind him and pushed up on the heavy load with her hands. After they had gone quite a way he said, "Now you must go home. Thank you. You are a good girl."

Hannele was happy that she had helped the old man, but then she looked down at the dress. It was very dirty from the black charcoal. And her hands too were black. She began to cry. She was afraid her mother would be very angry and she didn't know what to do. "How can I go home like this?" she thought.

As she sat on the stone crying, the sun went down and the moon came up. The moon saw the little girl crying, and the moon said, "Why are you crying?"

Hannele looked up in amazement. "I helped an old man with his load of charcoal, but now my dress is all dirty," she explained.

"Are you sorry about helping the old man?" asked the moon.

"Oh no," she said, "I know it was a good thing to do. But what shall I do about my lovely new dress—it's all dirty!" and she began to cry again.

"Get up," said the moon. "Go home now. I promise you your dress will be more beautiful than ever!" He sent rays of moonlight down on the spots, and each one turned into a little shiny jewel sewed on the dress. Hannele was very happy. She ran all the way home, and when she opened the door the whole house was full of light from the shiny little stars on her dress. Her mother exclaimed, "Hannele, what happened to you?" And Hannele told her the whole story.

(This makes a good playlet for children to act out.)

—Translated by Tamar Shachar and Ruth Brin

A Boy Named Chuckles:

A Story for Young Children

Long ago, a man named Abraham heard God calling to him. Abraham and his beautiful wife, Sarah, lived in a city in the East. But God told Abraham to leave the city with his wife and servants and go to live in a place called Canaan. He would have to live in a tent instead of a house. He would have to wander from one place to another with his flocks of animals, sheep and goats, instead of working in the city. But God promised that Abraham would become the father of a great people and that they would be a blessing to all other people.

So Abraham left the city, as God told him, and had many adventures as he wandered from place to place. But he grew old, and his wife, Sarah, was old, and they had no children. How could God keep his promise now, when Sarah was older than your grandmother, too old to have a baby?

One day three men came to Abraham's tent. In those days there were no motels for travelers. It was a rule to take care of strangers and travelers. But Abraham was kind, and he did more than follow the rule. He asked Sarah to make a feast for the men. She roasted a lamb from the flock and baked cakes for them, and they stayed in the tent. Then, while she was standing in the doorway, the men said, "We are messengers from God. At this time next year, we will come again, and Sarah will have a baby." When Sarah heard this, she began to laugh, because she thought she was too old, yet the idea made her happy. Abraham believed what the men had told him.

To Sarah's surprise, after a little while, she found

23

she was going to have a baby. When he was born, and he was a healthy little boy, she laughed again. In Hebrew that little boy's name was "Yitz-hak," which means "laughter." In English we call him Isaac. As God promised, he grew up to be the ancestor of the Jewish people. That is, this baby that we might call "Chuckles" was *your* great-great-great-great-great-great-great-great-great-grandfather!

Family Tree

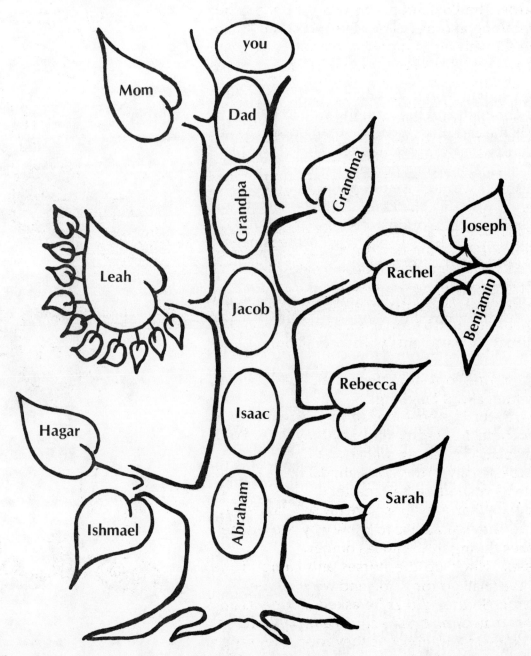

Laughter and Dancing:

A Chassidic Playlet for Children 6–12

NARRATOR: The Baal Shem Tov was a great teacher who lived long ago in Eastern Europe. One "Shabbas," he sat with his students at dinner. Everything was ready—the tablecloth was white, the candles were lit, and there was wine in the cups.

BAAL SHEM: *(Lifts his cup as if to begin to say the kiddush, but he breaks into merry laughter instead. Finally, when finished laughing, he sings the blessing.)*

FIRST STUDENT: *(Whispering)* Why did he laugh?

SECOND STUDENT: We have to wait until after Shabbas—we never bother him with questions on the Sabbath, you know.

NARRATOR: The meal went on, and everyone was happy, but they noticed that the master's eyes had a faraway look. Suddenly, he stopped eating his fish.

BAAL SHEM: *(Laughs again, even more loudly.)*

NARRATOR: And before the meal was over, right after the soup, he laughed a third time. After dinner and all day Saturday, the students whispered among themselves:

FIRST STUDENT: I looked in the Torah, but I couldn't find anything about laughing.

SECOND STUDENT: And I looked in the Talmud and the Zohar and I couldn't find anything. . . . Well, when Shabbas is over, we will ask him.

NARRATOR: Finally, after havdalah, darkness fell and the students rushed to their master.

BAAL SHEM: What questions have my scholars today?

STUDENT: They would like to know why you laughed three times during the Shabbas dinner.

BAAL SHEM: Hitch up the horses and climb in the wagon. We shall go for a ride and we shall see.

NARRATOR: So they did as he asked. *(Students and Baal Shem may climb on the couch and jiggle a bit as though riding in a wagon.)* As they rode, they sang a little song, and wandered through the night. *(Chil-*

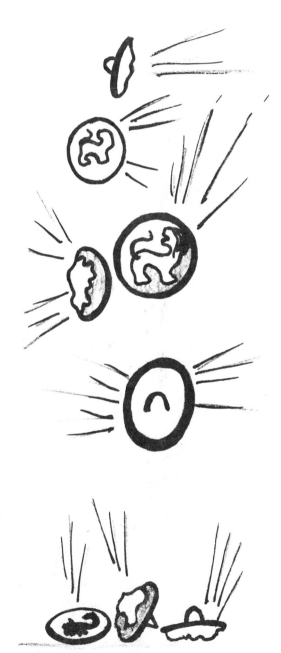

dren can sing here.) The next morning they came to a little village they had never seen before. They stopped in front of the synagogue, and soon many people gathered to see the famous Baal Shem. He looked about and asked:

BAAL SHEM: Which of you is Sabbatai, the book-binder?

NARRATOR: An old man stepped forward, followed by his wife.

BAAL SHEM: Now, tell me exactly what happened last Shabbas and what you did.

OLD MAN: I will, and if I did wrong, then let me be punished.

NARRATOR: The old man explained that he was a bookbinder and that long ago, when he was young, he had married the prettiest girl in the village. He had plenty of work and so they ate well, and he loved to buy her pretty clothes and to wear nice clothes himself and to go dancing.

OLD MAN: Perhaps that was wrong, but we were always good Jews too, and every Thursday, I gave my wife money to buy candles, flour, wine, meat, and all the things we needed for Shabbas. And every Friday, I closed my shop early and went to the synagogue to pray, and on the way home, I would see the candles twinkling brightly in my window. So it was for many years.

NARRATOR: But then, the old man said, they became old, there was less work, and less money, until finally, last Thursday, there was no money at all. For the first time, in all those years, she could not go to market to shop for the Sabbath. The old man was very sad.

OLD MAN: I told my wife that we would fast and pray for the Shabbas. But if our neighbors knew, they would bring us candles and fish and meat, and I didn't want to take charity. So I decided to be the last one to come home from the synagogue so no one would ask me why no candles were burning in my house.

OLD WOMAN: Meanwhile, I decided that I might as well clean my house again—there was no cooking to do. I shined the pots and pans and dusted everywhere. Then I remembered the chest in the attic full of our old clothes, and I thought I might as well take them out and air them and mend them. We might need to wear some of them soon.

OLD MAN: And that was when something exciting happened!

OLD WOMAN: In the old chest, I found a coat my husband used to wear when we went dancing. And on it were seven gold buttons. I snipped them off and ran to the goldsmith, and he weighed them and paid me—so off I ran to the market to buy everything I needed for Shabbas!

OLD MAN: And so when I left the synagogue, I saw the candles twinkling, and when I came home, the table was spread. But I was afraid my wife had asked the neighbors for help. I didn't want to embarrass her, but I was so curious, I gently asked what had happened.

OLD WOMAN: And then I told him! And there was even enough money left for food for two more days!

OLD MAN: Master, I was so overjoyed, that when I began to say the kiddush to praise the Lord and thank him, I took my wife by the hands and we began to dance in our little house and to laugh with joy.

OLD WOMAN: And when I served the fish, he was so happy, we danced again!

OLD MAN: And when she brought the soup, we laughed and danced a third time—we were so happy with the glory and goodness of God!

NARRATOR: Now the old man stopped speaking and hung his head.

OLD MAN: But master, if our dancing and laughter disturbed the peace of the Sabbath, I am truly sorry and we will fulfill any punishment you put upon us.

BAAL SHEM: Now listen to me—master bookbinder, and your wife, and all my scholars, and all the people of this village—I want you to know that all the angels in heaven sang and laughed and were joyful with this man and his wife . . . there was joy everywhere even in the Eternal Heart of God . . . and, for the three times you heard me laugh, my students, I was here with them when they laughed and danced, and I laughed and danced and sang with them! This was the true delight of Shabbas.

———

ALL: The Baal Shem laughed
The Baal Shem sang
The Baal Shem prayed
He took delight
in everything
that God has made.

Miriam:

A Story to Read to Little Children

Long ago, a little girl named Miriam lived in Egypt. Her father and mother had a small farm and a herd of cattle. But just after her brother, Aaron, was born, a new Pharaoh came to rule over Egypt. He said that all the Jews must be his slaves. Miriam's mother had to go to work cleaning the rooms in the palace. Her father had to help make bricks to build a huge silo where the Pharaoh would store his grain. Now Miriam had to take care of her little brother, and the days were long and hard for her. But at night, when her parents came home, they praised her. Her father told her stories about Joseph, and about Abraham and Sarah, and Isaac and Rebecca, and Jacob and Rachel. So Miriam learned about her people, and she began to wonder what would become of them.

Meanwhile, her mother, Jochabed, was going to have another baby. Miriam was very worried because she had heard that the wicked Pharaoh had decided that all Hebrew baby boys must be killed. By then, Miriam was almost twelve years old. She decided she would try to hide the baby if it was a boy, but she wasn't sure how she could do it. The soldiers sometimes came searching in the houses of the Hebrew slaves. Hers was just a one-room hut without any good hiding place for a baby.

When the child was born, it was a little boy. The first time she saw him, with his red, wrinkled face, Miriam wanted to cuddle him and take care of him. He was chubby, and in a few weeks he smiled at her. But she was afraid the soldiers would come, so she and her mother made a brave plan. Because Jochabed worked at the palace, she knew the place on the river where the Pharaoh's daughter went to swim every day. Maybe if the princess found a baby she would want to keep it. She was a kind lady, young and pretty.

So Miriam and her mother took a basket and made it waterproof with pitch and put soft blankets inside to wrap the baby. Then they floated the basket among the reeds on the Nile River, out of the current.

Miriam hid nearby in some bushes and watched. After a little while the princess and her maids came down to the water. When they stepped into the river, one of them saw the little basket.

"Look, Princess," she called, "here is a basket with a little baby inside!"

Miriam felt her heart beating hard. What would they do now? The maid picked the baby out of the basket and brought him to the princess.

"He's cute," the princess said, and poked his tummy. The baby kicked, then curled his tiny fist around her finger and smiled at her. The princess laughed. "Let's keep him!" she said, taking him in her arms, "maybe he's a Hebrew baby, but let's keep him anyway."

One of her women said, "But, Princess, how will you take care of such a little one? Babies are lots of trouble, you know."

Now Miriam, feeling very frightened, knew she must come out of her hiding place. She ran to the princess and knelt in front of her, "Please, your majesty," she said, "I know a servant in your palace that can take care of the little boy for you, and then you can play with him when you want to. Her name is Jochabed."

"Fine!" the princess tossed her head at the woman who had objected, "We'll call him Moses because we pulled him out of the water. You take him to this servant now and tell her to bring him to me in the morning." She gave Miriam her baby brother and turned away. Miriam ran to her mother with Moses in her arms.

Miriam knew that this little baby would grow up to be an important person. The Bible tells us that she was a prophetess, and so as she grew older she realized, long before Moses did, that he would be the one to lead the people out of Egypt and out of slavery. During all the troubled and exciting times when they were grown, he listened to her advice carefully, and she helped him lead the people in the wilderness.

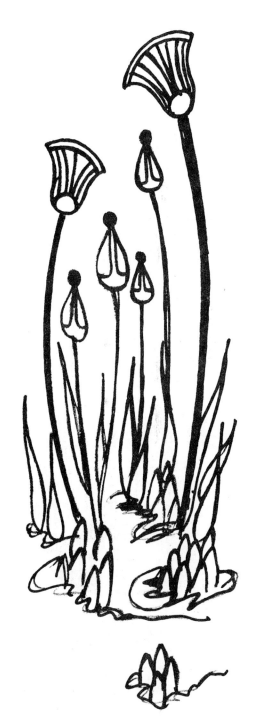

Brotherly Love:

The Joseph Stories Retold, for Older Children

Introduction

David Kossoff is a character actor and storyteller whose retellings of Bible stories on the BBC, starting in 1962, became so popular that they drew a huge audience. We are including our edited version of four chapters of the Joseph story, reprinted by kind permission of the Follett Publishing Company, Chicago.

We hope you have a storyteller or reader in your family who will read these stories aloud, so that everyone can enjoy them. One Sabbath theme is the strengthening of Jewish family life. What better illustration can be found than the story of Joseph? Beginning with some of the weaknesses of many families, such as favoritism toward children and jealousy among brothers, this story moves to a marvelous ending where Joseph, in spite of his years of slavery, is able to rescue his family from starvation. His love for his brothers and his father brings them all together again in a most moving scene. For adults Thomas Mann's *Joseph and His Brothers* is a classic of modern literature and a great retelling of the Biblical story.

Many Jewish families have experiences like these. In spite of family problems, there has been an important sense of loyalty and solidarity. In America, many immigrants who came first later sent for their brothers and sisters, ultimately rescuing whole groups from Nazi and Soviet terror. In Israel today, many families bring each other from the far corners of the earth, and where families have been destroyed, it is the Jewish people that play the role of Joseph, the brother who saves.

One way to use these stories is to tell your children how your own family came to the United States. Who helped them? To whom did they give help? Relate your own history to Jewish history. It is also possible to discuss how often Jews migrated from countries of danger to places of safety, and how family loyalty is a factor in Jewish survival. Almost any Jewish history will attest to this but you may want to refer to: Cecil Roth, *A History of the Jews* (Schocken paperback), and Frances Butwin, *The Jews of America* (Behrman House paperback).

Another kind of discussion which can flow from these stories is a discussion of intrafamily relationships. If your children are old enough, and if you feel it is wise to let them discuss their feelings of jealousy toward each other or their possible feeling that a parent or grandparent may favor or slight one child, you may encourage such a discussion. You may be guided by such books as *People Making* by Virginia Satir or *The Psychological World of the Teen Ager* by David Offer.

If your family has experienced divorce and there are half-brothers or step-sisters among your children, it may be interesting to note that the patriarchal families, like Jacob's, had children of one father and different mothers. Jacob had sons by his wives, Leah and Rachel, and by their handmaidens, his concubines, Bilhah and Zilpah. The status of the mothers did not affect the importance of the sons, who became the ancestors of the "twelve tribes of Israel" or "the children of Israel."

We are not encouraging you to enter into a discussion of this sort unless you feel your children are old enough, and that you and they could benefit from such frankness. If you can strengthen your family and move toward reconciliation through this experience, it is well worth while. Concentrate on the end of the story, to note that the brothers admitted their guilt and asked pardon, and that Joseph was abundantly and wholeheartedly forgiving, seeing good in all that had happened.

Incidentally, a family in Denver that participated in

SIGNS OF THE 12 TRIBES

31

Now
Jacob
Loved Joseph
More Than
All
His Children....
And
He Made Him
A
Coat
of Many Colors

Genesis 31:3

our project found this experience one of the most moving in the whole year. Their children were teen-agers.

Here are some questions which parents could use in discussing the Joseph stories, after reading them:

1. What kind of father was Jacob, when he made it obvious that Joseph was his favorite? On the other hand, sending Joseph alone to check on the welfare of his brothers may indicate some other feelings on Jacob's part.
2. Why does the Bible so often seem to favor the younger brother (Isaac over Ishmael, Jacob over Esau, Joseph over the other ten—only Benjamin was younger)? Why, in fact, is this a favorite theme in fairy tales? Is it because most people tend to identify with the less-favored or less-privileged "younger brother"? Or do you have some other interpretation?
3. How did Joseph handle his ambivalent feelings about his brothers? (Two kinds of feelings—he hated them for selling him into slavery—he loved them and wanted to rescue them and his father.) How do you think he felt when he ran into the other room and cried? Even though travel and communication were very difficult in those days, do you think Joseph should have communicated, or tried, with his father after he became a prince of Egypt? Do you feel, as Joseph said, that God planned the entire sequence of events?
4. Have you noticed examples where families that seem full of jealousies pull together in a real crisis and help each other, the way this family did?

The Joseph stories are divided into four chapters and can be read over a period of four weeks.

1. Brotherly Love

Now, you'd think that when Jacob had sons of his own, the one thing he'd certainly try to avoid was making the same mistake his Mother had made. After all, he had been Mother's boy and a lot of good it had done him—exiled, worked for years for an uncle he didn't like, without even being paid, afraid of his brother's revenge for twenty-five years. You'd think he'd have said, "I won't play favorites!"

But he did. He was worse than his mother. She had

twins, and she liked Jacob better than Esau. Jacob had thirteen children, twelve sons and a daughter, and the apple of his eye was Joseph. Joseph was the child of Rachel, Jacob's first true love. His first wife, Leah, and his two concubines all had had several children before Rachel, who after wanting a baby for many years finally had one. And that baby, the eleventh son, was called Joseph. She later had another son, Benjamin, making twelve in all for Jacob.

However, to get back to his father's favoritism for Joseph. Jacob's business was livestock—a huge business—cattle, sheep, goats, asses, camels, everything. Very rich man indeed. Not city people. They lived far out in the country. The boys grew up rough and tough. Jacob's sons were herdsmen and shepherds. Everybody had to work, but the younger sons worked a shorter day. Not that Jacob needed any excuse to keep his favorite near him. Jacob's word was law, and his love blinded him to the jealousy of his other sons. Joseph, mind you, *was* different from his brothers. He was gentle and quiet, clever, learned quickly, and was logical and pleasant. He enjoyed his life, and respected his father, and  grew into a handsome, well-built seventeen-year-old most people liked a lot. Most people—except his elder brothers couldn't stand him! But Joseph shut out their dislike by dreaming.

Yes, Joseph was a dreamer. A visionary. And his brothers made fun of him and laughed at what they called his dream talk. Sometimes, though, when he talked about his dreams at the evening meal, there was no laughter. Just a ring of dark, angry eyes. For his brothers realized that some of his dreams meant that someday they would all be servants, and Joseph would rule over them. Maybe it was God who was sending Joseph these dreams, but it would have helped if God had also sent him a little tact. Even old Jacob was rather put out once or twice by Joseph's dreams. But in Jacob's eyes, Joseph could do no wrong. Silly, really, for favoritism always causes trouble in families. Nearly everyone, including Joseph's brothers, wore clothes of rough cloth or animal skins, but Jacob gave Joseph a beautiful coat of very fine cloth of many different colors—and with sleeves. The brothers were furious. Nobody wore coats with sleeves except princes. What an idiotic present!

Jacob didn't notice the bad atmosphere, and one day he sent for Joseph. "I want you to go and see if all is well with your brothers," he said. "They are with the flock at Shechem." Joseph found that the flock and his brothers had moved on to a place called Dothan, about fifty miles from home. He had to walk, so it took a long time. His brothers spotted him coming before he saw them. They were hot and tired from working so hard, and the sight of Joseph in his bright-colored coat was just the last straw. "We'll kill him," they said. "We'll say a wild animal did it. We'll toss his body down a pit. Him and his dreams! Let's get rid of him for good!"

Now the oldest brother, Reuben, knew that Joseph's death would just about kill his father. So he tried to calm his brothers down. "No," said Reuben, "no killing. We'll just toss him in a pit for a day or two to teach him a lesson." (Reuben had a secret plan to pull Joseph out of the pit when his brothers moved on with the flocks.) The others listened to Reuben. When Joseph arrived, his brothers beat him up a little, but didn't really hurt him. Then they took his beautiful coat away from him and put him into a dry well with steep, smooth walls, and took the rope away.

Joseph lay there, bruised and sore. The well was pretty deep, and he couldn't hear any sounds from above. He had no idea what was going on. Good thing, too. For what was going on was all bad. Reuben had gone off to check how things were going with the sheep-shearing. His brothers stayed behind. They were just settling down to a meal when one of them, a quick-thinking man called Judah, looked up and saw a caravan of traders coming. He knew by the time of year that they would be on their way down to Egypt.

"Now listen," said Judah, "I've an idea that will get Joseph out of our hair for good. Reuben was right. Killing him would be wrong. So we won't kill him. We'll obey Reuben—and we'll make money! We'll sell him." His brothers looked at Judah. They knew he had a bad temper, but he wasn't crazy. And he was a sharp trader.

"Yes, we'll sell him," said Judah. He pointed to the approaching line of camels and men. "I know that lot; their main business is in oils and herbs. They do a lot in medicine-roots and skins and wool, too. But they'll deal in anything if the price is right—even slaves!

Well," he said—and he grinned like a wolf—"why don't we sell them a slave cheap?"

And it was done. Joseph was up out of the pit and stumbling away on stiff legs behind a camel before he knew what was happening. Judah and the other brothers divided the money and finished their meal. They laughed a lot and drank a lot and stayed up very late, and they all felt very clever.

The next day, Reuben came back. Judah, swaggering a bit, told him all about the deal and held out Reuben's tenth share to him. Reuben stood very still and looked at his brothers. "Very clever," he said, "thank you for telling me. Have you decided yet which one of you will tell our father?" Suddenly nobody wanted to look at anybody else. "This will just about kill the old man," said Reuben. "Joseph was the favorite, and we didn't like him, but this is a terrible thing we've done."

Judah was now very ashamed. "Well, *you* don't have to tell him," he said, "you weren't here." Reuben looked at Judah. "Now listen," said Judah. "We won't tell Dad the truth; we'll kill a goat and smear the blood on Joseph's coat. We'll tear the coat, too, and we'll tell Dad we found it on our way back. Joseph left home after we did and traveled alone. Dad will think he was killed and eaten by wild animals."

Well, the news did nearly kill old Jacob. Nobody could comfort him. He sat with the torn and blood-stained coat across his knees and wept and mourned. A light had gone from his life. He didn't know, of course, that the light had not gone out. It had gone to Egypt.

2. Joseph the Slave

Well, there stood Joseph—in a slave market in Egypt. His feet were blistered and raw. He was filthy and thirsty and exhausted. He had been walking for days and days. And now he was up for sale. Fairly high price, for he was young, and well-built, and smart. The traders were offering him for sale as a house-servant, not a field-slave or laborer. Joseph stood still, and as straight as he could. He closed his eyes against the bright sun. When he opened them again he saw a tall, handsome man wearing a soldier's uniform. He was the captain of Pharaoh's personal guard. His name was Potiphar. He was used to judging the quality of men at first glance. He asked the price, paid it, and walked away. Joseph was delivered to the officer's home within the hour. He was fed and given a small room and new clothes. He bathed, and shaved, and slept like a log for almost a whole day.

He was adaptable, was Joseph, and made the best of things. He was optimistic, and always had a strong feeling God was on his side. Wasn't far wrong, either. God had biggish plans for Joseph and got started right away. Potiphar began to find he'd bought a great bargain in his new house-servant. This Joseph could read and write, and had a fine, logical mind. Left to handle something tricky, he used good judgment. He could handle men without raising his voice. Soon Potiphar left more and more to Joseph. His household had never been so well run. Eventually Potiphar made Joseph head man. In charge of everything. He really liked Joseph, and treated him almost like a son.

Potiphar's wife, however, had different ideas. Very pretty, she was, and much younger than her husband. She also appreciated her beautifully run household and her perfectly cooked meals and her well-trained staff. She also appreciated her overseer. And who wouldn't? Joseph was now in his early twenties. Tall, dark, and very handsome. He treated his master's wife with perfect manners and great respect. Which was the last thing she wanted. She didn't want perfect manners and great respect. She wanted Joseph! She tried every trick she knew, but Joseph was grateful to Potiphar and was a loyal and honorable man. Well, the lady turned nasty. She stole one of Joseph's robes, had it found in her room, and told a lot of lies about how he was in love with her, and had come to her room, and how she'd fought bravely, and how he'd fled, leaving his robe behind—a very silly story. But often the most unlikely stories are believed, and this lady was a first-class liar.

Well, Potiphar believed it; every word. And he threw Joseph into prison.

The years went by. Prison wasn't too bad. Just lately Joseph had been thinking a lot about dreams and their meanings, and about God, who seemed to be in his dreams a lot, and who seemed to put the clear meanings of his dreams into Joseph's mind. You'll notice, though, that having God for a close friend didn't necessarily mean it was going to be roses all the way.

Anyway, there he was in the king's prison—that is, in Pharaoh's prison. A better class of people than ordinary prisons. Joseph had been in prison quite a while now. Four to five years. There'd been no trial or anything. It all depended on the king, whether you got out or not, and the king didn't even know Joseph was there. It was Potiphar, remember, the king's captain of the guard, who'd put Joseph away. But Joseph wasn't complaining. The pattern had repeated itself. He was now right-hand man to the chief jailer. He pretty well ran the place. He knew every prisoner, and they all liked and trusted him. He always had time for people, that's why. If you were troubled, you told your troubles to Joseph, and the trouble right away seemed to get smaller, and if you had a bad dream, Joseph could explain it so it might turn out to have a quite unfrightening meaning.

Well, one morning there was some excitement. Two men from the king's private household were admitted to prison. Pharaoh's chief baker, and Pharaoh's chief butler. How they'd offended the king with their buttling and baking we don't know, but there they were—prisoners. Both a bit scared and both turning, as everyone did, to Joseph to cheer them up. Months passed, and Joseph got to know the butler and the baker pretty well, and from them heard a lot about the king—Pharaoh, that is—and his court. The butler and the baker talked a lot about how the king had a custom of forgiving wrongdoers to celebrate his birthday. They didn't much want to talk about what they'd done to make Pharaoh so mad, but they were setting a lot of store on getting a birthday pardon. Three days before the birthday, they both came to Joseph, pretty upset. They'd both had very exciting dreams, and they'd heard that Joseph could interpret dreams—that is, tell them what the dreams meant. Joseph listened as always, quiet and sympathetic. He waited until he felt sure that God was there handling the dreams department, and then he turned first to the butler.

"The vine and its three branches and the grapes and wine in your dream mean that Pharaoh will forgive you in three days, and you'll get your old job back. You'll be in charge of the king's table and the king's wine again." The butler was overjoyed, and promised to put in a word for Joseph to get him pardoned, too. "Leave it to me," he said, "I won't forget!"

Joseph now turned to the baker, sort of a ratlike, shifty type; word was out that he had run a racket with stolen flour and wheat. "Well," said the little man, "good for me, too?" Joseph felt sad. "Er . . . no," he said. "Your life will change in three days too. There will be no pardon for you. I don't know what you did to make Pharaoh angry, but you will be hanged for it." And he was.

3. Dreams Come True

Well, the butler forgot his promise. People do. But about two years later, God jogged his memory. Pharaoh, king of Egypt, was quite a nice man. Bit of a worrier. Superstitious. Believed in all sorts of nonsense. The palace was absolutely littered with idols and gods. But this particular morning the king was getting no comfort from any of them. He was seated, as is only right, on his throne, and around him were about two dozen of the top magicians and wise men in Egypt. They all sat there, nobody talking. Then the king spoke.

"I brought you all here," he said, "at considerable expense; you've been here about a week and a half, and you've come up with nothing. I brought you here to interpret two dreams; I've had them twice more since you've been here. You've told me nothing but rubbish!"

Then the king turned to his butler. "Stop fidgeting," he said. "Stand still. What's the matter, anyway?"

The butler came nearer. "My lord," he said, "I've just remembered something that may help. Remember about two years ago, when I made you cross about something and you threw me into the palace jail?" "So?" said the king. "On my birthday I forgave you, and you got your job back."

"Ah, yes," said the butler, "but the baker you threw into jail with me. You hanged him. Same day. On your birthday." "So?" said the king.

"Well," said the butler, "the baker and I knew what you were going to do to us three days *before* your birthday."

"No one knew," the king said. "I didn't make up my mind until after I opened my presents."

"But we knew," said the butler. "A prisoner interpreted our dreams. A young man he was. In charge of other prisoners. A Hebrew. Name of Joseph. I promised to say a word for him, but I forgot. I feel bad about it."

"So you should," said the king. "Get Joseph and bring him here." And very soon Joseph stood before Pharaoh. He stood quietly, waiting for God to help him know what Pharaoh's dreams meant. Finally he got that familiar "sure" feeling and began to speak. "The two dreams are one dream," Joseph said. "Two messages from my God. The real God. There's only one, and he's doing you a great favor. He has told you what's coming. It is this. There will be seven years of great plenty, rich crops, plenty of food for everybody. But then there will be seven years of famine, starving."

Pharaoh sat very still. "I knew it was bad," he said. "Does your God send any other message?"

Joseph went on. "Appoint overseers in every part of the land to gather and store one-fifth of every crop of grain. Build great storehouses; plant more grain; encourage better farming. All overseers to be in charge of local area managers. State marshals in charge of overseers. All marshals report to one man. That man Pharaoh shall appoint. End of message."

Pharaoh took a gold chain from his neck and put it on Joseph's neck. "You are the man," he said. "Your God is no fool. Stay to dinner. You start work tomorrow."

Well, another ten years passed. Everything Joseph told Pharaoh would happen did happen. There were seven years of rich crops, and now it is the middle of the seven years of famine. God's advice, which Joseph passed on to Pharaoh, is working. A first-class rationing system is in operation. Nobody gets fat, but nobody is starving. Joseph has been in charge of everything. He is now forty years old. He is married and has two small sons. He is a tall, handsome man who lives and looks like what he is—an Egyptian prince. Joseph by now had lived half his life in Egypt. He didn't often remember the first half of his life. When he did, it was with mixed feelings. He remembered the love of Jacob, his father. He remembered his jealous brothers sold him to slavers. He remembered only one brother with real warmth.

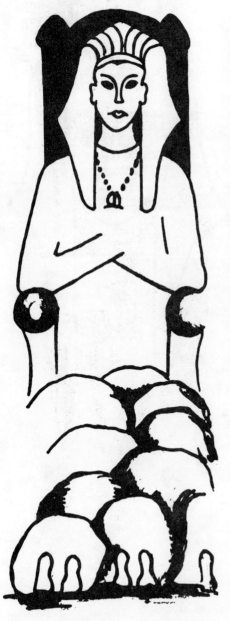

That was his younger brother Benjamin, the baby of the family. Just lately Joseph had been wondering whether the famine was bad in Canaan, where his father and brothers lived. At least he thought they were still alive. He'd had no contact with them for twenty years; it was a long way to Canaan by camel, maybe four hundred miles.

Well, that very day Joseph was to find out. Three times a week the storehouses sold grain to people not covered by the rationing system, wandering desert tribes and such. Joseph made it a point to look in on these deals. When he got there on the morning I'm speaking of, a group of ten men were waiting. Joseph knew them at once. They were his brothers. He counted again quickly. No Benjamin. The brother he most wanted to see again was not with them. The ten brothers bowed low before Joseph. Nothing about this richly dressed Egyptian with his gold ornaments and badges of office and his black wig reminded them of the seventeen-year-old brother they'd sold as a slave. They had come, they told Joseph, to buy grain, because their families were starving. They said they were from Canaan, the sons of Jacob. Now Joseph had no reason to love his brothers, but he was not vengeful. However, seeing his other brothers made him want to see Benjamin even more. After Reuben, the eldest brother, finished speaking, Joseph waited in silence for a while, and then spoke.

"Because I fear God," he said, "he gives me special knowledge, and so I know that there are twelve sons of Jacob, not ten."

The brothers were thunderstruck. Reuben was the first to be able to speak. "Lord," he said, "our father indeed had twelve sons; the youngest is at home with him, the other . . . "

"The other?" said Joseph.

Poor Reuben, who hadn't even been there when Joseph had been sold, and who was really the best of the bunch, was ashamed, and afraid, too, of this magical person. At last he said, "The other . . . is no more."

Joseph left another silence. His mind was now made up. "All right," he said, "fill your bags with grain and pay in silver. Provisions will be given you for your return journey. One of you will stay here in

prison until you bring your youngest brother to me."
Joseph rose from his throne, and just couldn't resist
adding, "And I know also from God that the brother
you will bring back is called Benjamin." Well, you can
just imagine.

4. A Different Judah

The brothers went back to Canaan, and as usual it was
Reuben's job to tell their old father the bad news, that
his son Simeon was in Pharaoh's prison and would
stay there until his brothers brought Benjamin to
Egypt. "Fantastic the way that tall Egyptian knew all
about us!" they added. When Reuben finished his
story, old Jacob sat quiet. Then he said, "And you say
that when you opened the bags of grain your money
was inside, too? It is beyond understanding. I do not
want Benjamin to go. Joseph went once on a journey,
and he was eaten by wild beasts. I cannot risk my
Benjamin's life. Who knows what this Egyptian wants
of us?"

Well, weeks went by and the grain was all used, and
the old man called his sons together. "There is still
famine in the land," he said, "and only from Egypt
can we buy grain. If it must be, it must. Benjamin shall
go. Take gifts of fruits of the land, and take back the
money that was returned to you, and more money for
the new purchases. And I will pray that God will look
after us all."

When the brothers arrived at Joseph's great palace,
they were given fresh clothing and told to get cleaned
up because they were to lunch with the master. At
noon the master, Joseph, entered his great dining
room, where his brothers waited. The brothers
bowed low. Joseph told them to rise. Benjamin, who
was Joseph's full brother because they had had the
same mother, Rachel—the other brothers, remember, were only half-brothers, because they had
different mothers—felt an odd closeness to this
splendidly dressed Egyptian prince. He was sensitive,
was Benjamin, and felt somehow that the prince was
very nervous, near to tears almost. He wasn't far
wrong.

Joseph beckoned him forward. "You are Benjamin," he said. "Tell me, how is your father?" But
before Benjamin could answer, the prince rushed out
of the room. Poor Joseph! He was in tears. He longed

41

to say who he was, but it wasn't the right time yet. After a minute or two he calmed down, wiped his eyes, and went back to his guests. They hadn't moved. Joseph, aware of the many servants watching, watched himself, and lunch was served.

When the banquet was over, the brothers, including Simeon, who had been released from prison, set off for home. But Joseph wasn't finished with them. They'd gone just a little way when they heard the sound of horses' hooves behind them. It was a party of armed men, with orders to search the brothers' baggage for a valuable silver goblet missing from the great dining hall where they'd had lunch. The brothers were frightened, and when the goblet turned up in Benjamin's grain sack, they were even more frightened. They knew it was a frame-up, and there was nothing they could do. The brothers were surrounded and taken back to the city. Soon they stood before Joseph again.

"The goblet," said Joseph, "was mighty Pharaoh's and a gift to me. To steal from Pharaoh is to die. But in this case the thief shall be made a slave to serve me. Forever." He pointed at Benjamin. "This one is guilty; the others may go free."

Then Joseph waited. He wondered which brother would speak first. They all seemed shocked, dazed. Then Judah stepped forward. It was Judah, the wild, violent Judah, who had been the leader in selling Joseph to the slavers. "My Lord," he said, "we know that Benjamin is innocent. If anyone is to be punished, it should be the rest of us, not him, for long ago we sinned against God and against our father. This Benjamin is the son of our father's old age, and the only son left of Rachel, our father's true love. Our father would die if we return without Benjamin, as we once, long ago, returned without Joseph. My Lord," said Judah, "take me for a slave, and let Benjamin go."

At this point Joseph broke down. He wept. He told them who he was—and the joy and happiness are impossible to describe. He told them not to be ashamed, and he forgave them. "It was God's will," he said. "God sent me to Egypt to save you and many others from the famine. God showed me how to make the fat years provide for the lean. God made me as great as the king. Go," said Joseph, "and bring your families and all you own here to Egypt. And give my love to my father, and bring him, too. Tell him that Pharaoh has offered the most fertile land in Egypt for Israel and his children to live in."

The brothers went home with Joseph's message. Jacob wiped away his tears. "It is enough," he said, "Joseph is alive. I will see him again before I die." And the great gathering-together began, of all the Israelites and their possessions, and at last the huge cavalcade was on its way to Egypt.

Suggested Story Books for Young Children

A list of storybooks about Shabbat for children 3–6 to read at bedtime (one mother suggests that one parent read while the other puts the Friday meal on the table).

Favorites

Althea Silverman, *Habibi and Yow* (Bloch Publishing Company).
Sadie Weilerstein, *K'tonton* (Jewish Publication Society).

Others

Jane Bearman, *Good Shabbos* (Union of American Hebrew Congregations (UAHC).
Sophie Cedarbaum, *The Sabbath: A Day of Delight* (UAHC).
Mollie Cone, *Hear O Israel* (UAHC).
Morris Epstein, *My Holiday Story Book* (KTAV).
Robert Garvey, *Good Shabbas Everybody* (United Synagogue Commission on Jewish Education).
Robert Garvey, *Holidays are Nice* (KTAV).
Robert Garvey, *The First Book of Jewish Holidays* (KTAV).
Robert Garvey, *A Wonderful Shabbot* (KTAV)
Betty Hollender, *Bible Stories for Little Children* (UAHC).
Sol Scharfstein, *My First Book of Prayers* (KTAV).
Norma Simon, *Every Friday Night* (United Synagogue Commission).
Sadie Weilerstein, *What the Moon Brought* (Jewish Publication Society).

For Older Children, 6–10

H. Chanover, *My Book of Prayer* (United Synagogue).
David Einhorn, *The Seventh Candle* (KTAV).
Morris Epstein, *All About Jewish Holidays and Customs* (KTAV).
Leonard Jaffe, *Pitzel Holiday Book* (KTAV).
Ruth Samuels, *Bible Stories for Jewish Children: 1, 2* (KTAV).
Menachem Stern, *The Sun and the Clouds* (KTAV).

2

Dialogues for Children and Adults

A Shabbat Seder on the Theme of Creation

Especially for Families with Children Ages 6–13

MOTHER (or entire family): Blesses candles. Boruch ata Adonai, Elohenu melech ha-olam, asher kidshanu b'mitzvotov, vitzivanu l'hadlik ner shel shabbat. Blessed art Thou, O Lord our God, King of the universe, Who hast hallowed us by Thy commandments and commanded us to kindle the Sabbath light. (Or: We praise You, O Lord our God, Master of the universe, who has taught us the way of holiness through Your commandments, and has commanded us to light the Sabbath lights.)

בָּרוּךְ אַתָּה יְיָ, אֱלֹהֵינוּ מֶלֶךְ הָעוֹלָם, אֲשֶׁר קִדְּשָׁנוּ בְּמִצְוֹתָיו וְצִוָּנוּ לְהַדְלִיק נֵר שֶׁל שַׁבָּת.

YOUNGER CHILD: Mother, why do we light candles every Friday night?

MOTHER: The first thing God did, when he began creating the world, was to create light. He said, "Let there be light," and there was light. We have to have candles and matches, or electric lights, but the wonderful thing is that we can make light too. And so we can remember that God created the world. He created it out of nothing. That is the way God can create. When we want to make something, we have to start not only with an idea, but also with something from the world of nature, the world that God made.

FATHER: (Sings kiddush.) Boruch ata Adonai, Elohenu melech ha-olam, boray p'ri hagofen. Blessed art Thou, O Lord our God, master of the universe, who createst the fruit of the vine.

בָּרוּךְ אַתָּה יְיָ, אֱלֹהֵינוּ מֶלֶךְ הָעוֹלָם, בּוֹרֵא פְּרִי הַגָּפֶן.

YOUNGER CHILD: Why do we always have wine on Friday night? We don't have it other nights.

FATHER: Because wine comes with a delicious meal, and it means we are going to be happy together and enjoy the Sabbath and rest on this day. God rested on the seventh day, after He created the world and all living things. Wine and a good dinner help us give thanks to God for all his gifts, and remind us that this is the beginning of our day of rest.

OLDER CHILD: I know the motzi for the bread and I will say it. *Boruch ata Adonai Elohenu melech ha-olam ha motzi lechem min ha-oretz.* Blessed art Thou, O Lord our God, master of the universe, who brings forth bread from the earth.

ADULT: Why do you say that God brings forth bread from the earth? What about the farmer that grows the grain and the miller that makes the flour and the baker that bakes the bread?

OLDER CHILD: You and Mother already explained that! God created the earth and the sun and the rain and the seed, didn't He? The millers ground the flour, and Mother and I baked the bread out of the things God gave us. I think we worked with God, together, like partners.

ADULT: And I think you have said the most important thing of all: that man is God's partner in creation, and God is man's partner in the rest and joy and love we all want to feel on Shabbat.

EVERYONE: Shabbat Shalom.

בָּרוּךְ אַתָּה יְיָ, אֱלֹהֵינוּ מֶלֶךְ הָעוֹלָם, הַמּוֹצִיא לֶחֶם מִן הָאָרֶץ.

48

A Shabbat Seder on Prayer

For Adults and Children ages 6–13

ALL: *Sing or recite blessings for candles, wine, and bread.*

CHILD: All the prayers start *Baruch ata*. What does that mean, anyway? I don't really know what "Blessed art Thou" means in English.

ADULT: It means that God is praised by us and thanked by us. Translating from Hebrew to English is often difficult. *Baruch* is actually related to the Hebrew word which means "to kneel." We kneel to God, to praise and thank Him for a real thing we have in front of us—light, bread, wine, and for the good things they stand for: a happy home, food, the Sabbath, everything God gives us.

CHILD: Is that what prayer is, saying thanks? Can't we ask for things?

ADULT: Yes, we can ask God for things in prayer. We often do. Sometimes when you ask me for something I say to you, "Do you really need that?" And I ask you to think about what you need and what other people in the family need. Sometimes you even change your mind after you think about it. When we thank God, or when we ask for things in prayer, we try to think about what is really important. We try to judge ourselves and our request in God's eyes. And we don't always get what we ask for.

CHILD: But we keep on asking.

ADULT: Right, and we keep on praying. But on Shabbat, we try to avoid asking God for things because both man and God rest on Shabbat. We try to carry out the commandment—or mitzva—to love God. And when you love someone, it is natural to thank him for the things he does for you.

CHILD: I think it makes everybody feel good when you say thank you. Besides, it makes you happy to think about all the good things you already have, instead of thinking about what you want and don't have.

ADULT: You are right! It is always good to count our blessings. You know we are commanded to love God. Let's read this together out loud. It tells us what it means to love God and to pray to Him.

ALL: I can begin with a prayer of gratitude for all that is holy in my life. God may not need words, in English or Hebrew, but I need them.

Through prayer, I can sense my inner strength, my inner purpose, my inner joy, my capacity to love.

As I reach upward in prayer, I sense those qualities in my Creator.

To love God is to love the world He created and to work to perfect it.

To love God is to love my fellow-man and to work to make our lives better

To love God is to love the dreams of joy and peace that glow within all of us, and to work toward their fulfillment.

The Tabernacle in the Wilderness

A Dialogue for Adults and Children Age 7 and up

FIRST CHILD: I think it's scary when you move from one house to another. But when Moses took the children of Israel out of Egypt, they had to leave their houses and live out in the desert.

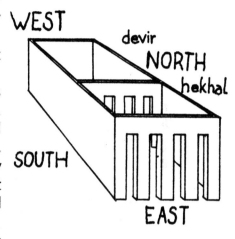

SECOND CHILD: I don't think that would be scary—it would be like a big camping trip or a pack trip.

FIRST ADULT: The Bible says they were sometimes frightened and that they complained quite a bit too. Still, it was something like a camping trip that lasted forty years. They had animals with them—sheep, goats, donkeys, and camels. They may have had a few wagons, but there were no roads, so they wouldn't have been much good. Most of what they carried had to go on their backs, or the animals' backs.

FIRST CHILD: They got manna, so they didn't have to carry much food. But what did the animals eat?

SECOND ADULT: They probably found something to graze on at the oases along the way—Bedouin people live in the Sinai desert today with herds. But when they traveled from one oasis to another, they had to carry water.

FIRST ADULT: They carried their possessions from Egypt—musical instruments (for example, Miriam danced with timbrels), clothing, and jewelry.

FIRST CHILD: How do you know they had jewelry? I thought they were poor slaves.

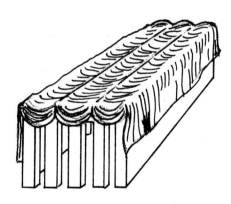

FIRST ADULT: They were given gifts by the Egyptians when they finally left—and they brought gold for the building of the golden calf, and afterwards, more importantly, for the building of the tabernacle, or mishkan.

SECOND ADULT: After Moses came down from Sinai with the stone tablets of the Ten Commandments they put them in an ark—a wooden box covered with gold—and they built a mishkan, or tabernacle, where they kept the ark. Around it was a courtyard walled off by curtains held up by poles, where the people could gather. When they moved, they carried it all with them. Also when they moved, the tabernacle remained in the center, and the twelve tribes traveled in a square, three on each side, surrounding it.

SECOND CHILD: It must have been very slow going with all those people and herds, and keeping in formation all the way. But I always thought the tabernacle was a tent, and this model we made looks a lot different—it's more box-shaped.

FIRST ADULT: This is close to the written description in the Bible, but we don't know exactly what it looked like. It was an ancient kind of tent. It was considered a holy place and called "the tent of meeting," meaning it was the place where Moses could go to meet God. An important thing is that this tabernacle was always in the center of the tribes, a symbol of their relationship to God.

FIRST CHILD: Sometimes you say God created the world, and then you say He met people in a little tent in the desert. How can that be?

SECOND ADULT: That's a question grown-ups ask as much as children do. Our traditions teach that God is the God of creation, but God is also the God of exodus. That means He not only started the whole universe, He is acting in it and in human history. At that time the children of Israel believed they could meet with God in that little tent, and Moses did.

FIRST ADULT: But today we are less sure of how God acts in history, and we don't know for sure where we can meet Him. We have to keep searching for Him.

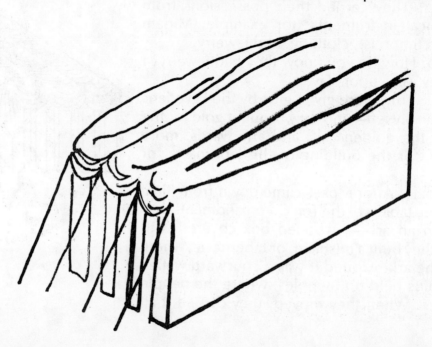

Havdalah:

A Dialogue for Children and Adults

If you are performing the service for the first time, you may want to read these questions afterwards.

FIRST CHILD: Why do we bless spices?

FIRST ADULT: No one seems to be sure how this pleasant custom started. Some say that on the Sabbath a man has an extra soul, or an extra angel hovering over him, to guard his rest. This higher soul —this angel—flies away on the fragrance of the spices.

SECOND CHILD: Why do we use a twisted candle, or two candles?

SECOND ADULT: The Hebrew says we thank God for the "lights of the fire," and since that is plural, we need more than one wick. Personally, I think we like to make a big light because the room is getting dark.

FIRST CHILD: Why did you ask me to hold the candle as high as I could?

FIRST ADULT: There is a legend that if a girl is holding the candle, the man she marries will be as tall as she reaches. If a boy holds the candle, he will grow to be as tall as he can reach. Do you like that idea?

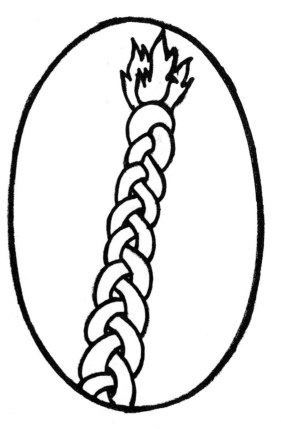

SECOND CHILD: Why do we bless the lights?

FIRST ADULT: I know one explanation. Light was the first thing created by God, so we must begin the week with it.

FIRST CHILD: I know another reason. We need fire for cooking and making lights and making tools to work with, so now that the Sabbath is over, we can use it again.

SECOND CHILD: I like havdalah because you can see the fire, smell the spices, and taste the grape juice—besides, you feel the warmth of the fire and have a good feeling about the new week!

53

3
Arts, Crafts, Games, Activities

Noah's Ark

Supplies Needed

- corrugated cardboard
- scissors
- quick-drying glue
- straight pins
- pencil
- ruler
- waxed paper

Making the Ark

(See pages 57, 58 for the ark pattern.)

1. Draw pattern on cardboard to sizes indicated, cut the pieces out, and draw the lines down the center of the hull bottom and the deck.
2. Lay the hull bottom flat on the table, which has been covered with newspaper. The center line should face up. Put quick-drying glue along the straight edge of the keel, and place perpendicular to the hull bottom along the center line. Let glue dry.
3. Glue the deck to the top of the keel along the center line of the deck. Let dry.
4. Slightly bend the hull sides to fit the curves of the deck and hull bottom. Put glue on the edges of the deck and hull bottom, working one side at a time. Form the hull sides along the edges of deck and bottom, holding in place with straight pins. When glue is dry, remove pins.
5. Glue the back edges of deck, sides, bottom, and keel, and place the stern with the narrow edge up.
6. Construct the cabin separately and glue onto the deck.

The Cabin

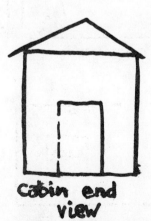

cabin end view

1. Cut a strip of cardboard 3 inches wide and 16 inches long. Measure the sides of the cabin as illustrated on page 57. Fold on fold lines and glue edges together.
2. Cut a square piece of cardboard 5 inches by 5 inches, and fold in half for a pitched roof. Put glue on the top edges of the cabin and wait until the glue is tacky. Place roof on top of cabin so that there is a ¾ inch overhang.
3. Put glue along bottom edge of cabin, and place on top of the deck toward bow of the ark.

You may now paint the ark or draw on it with felt pens.

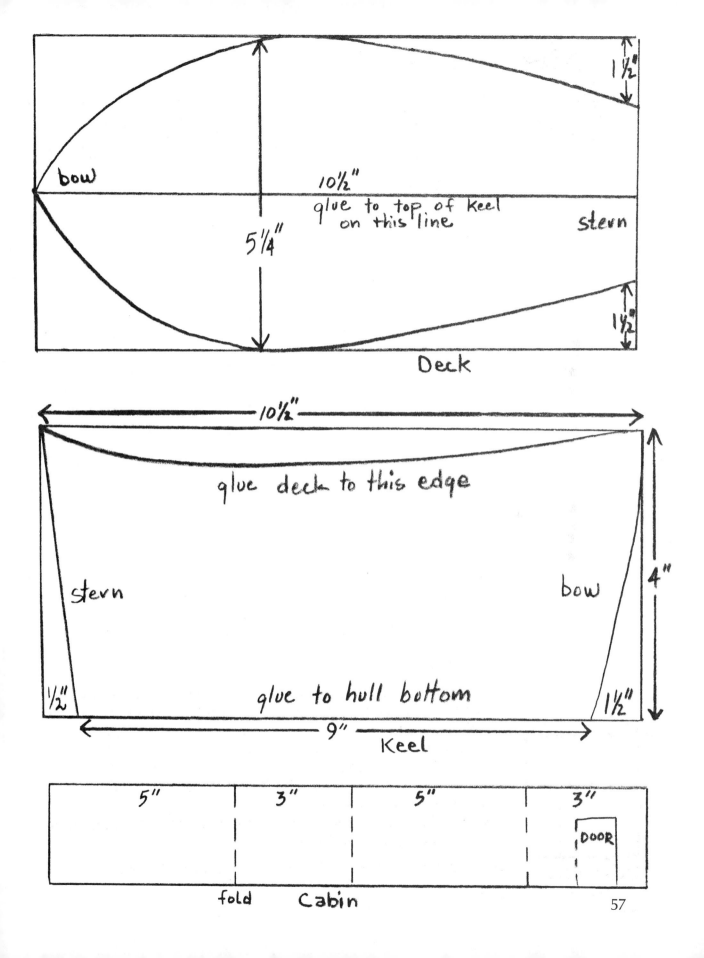

bow

10½"
glue to top of keel
on this line

stern

5¼"

1½"

1½"

Deck

10½"

glue deck to this edge

stern

bow

4"

½"

glue to hull bottom

1½"

9"

Keel

5"   3"   5"   3"

DOOR

fold   Cabin

57

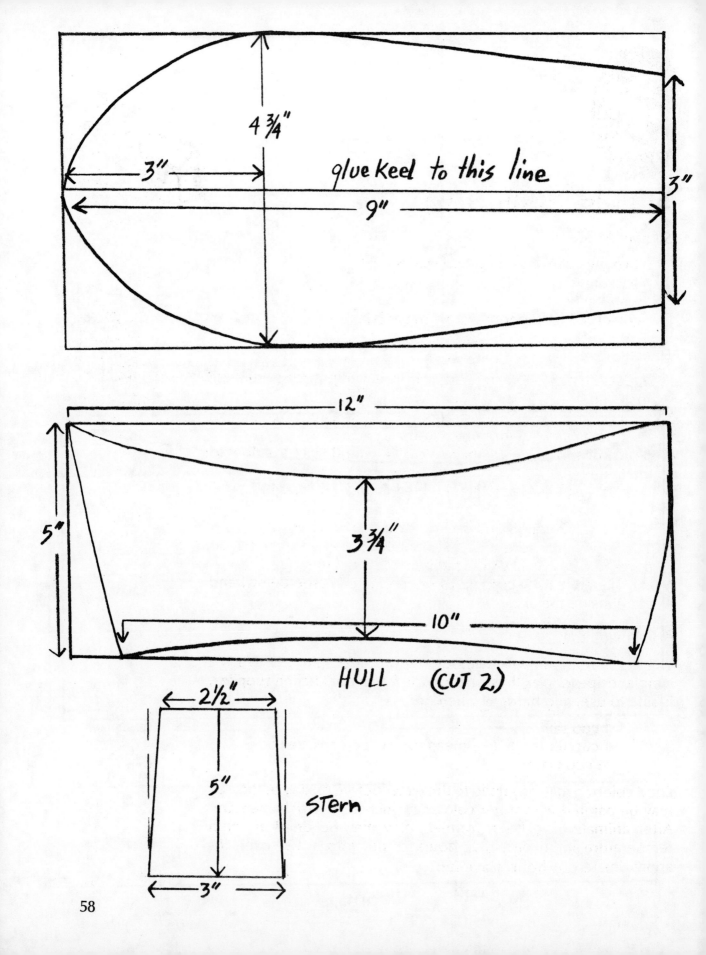

4 ¾"

glue keel to this line

3"

9"

3"

12"

5"

3 ¾"

10"

HULL   (CUT 2)

2½"

5"

Stern

3"

58

Simple Noah's Ark

Supplies Needed

    two milk cartons—½ gallon size is best
    scissors
    white glue
    construction paper or brown paper bag

Directions

1. Cut one side out of a milk carton, leaving the pointed end intact *(a)*.
2. Lay carton flat with open side up, and cut a rectangular door *(b)* from the top edge of the carton.
3. A cardboard ramp *(c)* may be cut to extend from the door to the table top.
4. Cabin—cut the bottom ⅓ off the second milk carton *(d)*.
5. Make a door *(e)* in one side.
6. Place carton open end *(d)* into carton *(a)* as shown.
7. Paint will not adhere to the waxed surface. This ark can be covered with construction paper and white glue.
8. Make animals according to recipe for clay (see below) and store inside the ark.

Homemade Clay

The ark is not complete without "two of every kind." Here is a simple recipe for clay that can be made from your kitchen supplies, is safe to use, and hardens when dry.

    1 cup salt
    1 cup flour   knead until even consistency
    ½ cup water

Food coloring may be added to the water before mixing or the clay may be painted with water colors, acrylics, or enamel when dry. After animals have been formed, they may be dried at room temperature for twenty-four hours or put into a 250° oven for approximately ½ hour. Have fun!

Paper Dolls for the Joseph Stories

To make the Joseph stories fun for small children, they could be told by an adult or older child as the younger ones act out the situations with this figure. Use as many characters in the story as you would like.

Cut this figure out of cardboard.

To act out the enclosed story using this paper doll, you will need thirteen figures; one for Jacob, and one for each of his twelve sons.

The gown can either be colored or covered with cloth. The gown of Joseph should be distinctly different from the others. Yarn or garment trim could be glued to the gown to make it especially colorful.

The figures can be used in paper-doll fashion by cutting the gown with tabs at the top.

The figures could be made to stand by attaching a popsicle stick to the figure and standing it in a hunk of playdough or other similar substance.

Draw the facial features on with a magic marker or pen. Hair and beards can be made out of yarn simply by glueing loops of yarn to the head and face as shown. Different colors may be used if desired.

Embroidered Challah Cover

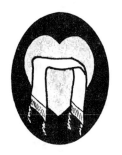

Disposable challah covers can be made by small children. They enjoy doing it while mom is preparing the dinner. Moms enjoy it too! Buy a box of large embossed paper napkins. Using crayons, the children can color in the designs of the embossing.

If you enjoy embroidery, here is a pattern for an embroidered challah cover. Only two stitches are suggested with the directions. However, many other stitches could be used effectively.

Supplies Needed

> material 13 inches x 13 inches (any kind of material can be used; cotton or linen blend would be nice)
> embroidery hoop
> scissors
> needle
> embroidery thread

Instructions

Cut the fabric into a square 13 inches by 13 inches. This will allow for a ⅝ inch hem. The drawing on the lower left side shows the finished piece. Draw the border and grape pattern onto the fabric using carbon paper and the pattern on page 72. The challah can be drawn on or omitted. White thread on white fabric is nice, or you can select colors of your choice. The stitches are easier to do if the fabric is stretched over an embroidery hoop. After the pattern is finished, iron the fabric flat and hem the edges.

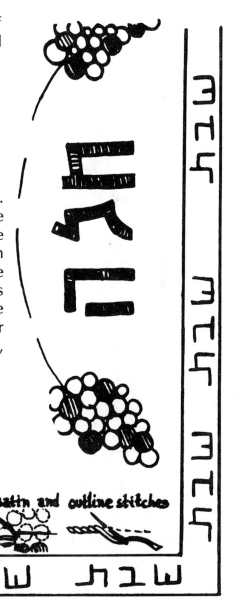

use satin and outline stitches

Candlemaking

If you wish to make your own candles, a fine project for adults and children to do together, here are the instructions:

There are basically three ways of making candles (at least for Jewish ceremonial purposes): (1) dipping, (2) rolling thin sheets of wax, (3) burning oil.

For candles you need:

1. Mold—a paper cup, food containers like milk cartons or yogurt containers, juice cans, glasses, etc.
2. Wick—available at crafts stores; heavy cotton twine can be used but candle wicking is preferable.
3. Paraffin—available at crafts stores or even at some supermarkets (look for boxes of Gulfwax).
4. Coloring agents—dyes available at crafts stores, or crayons (although these do not produce a true color).
5. A couple of small pots.
6. Optional are scents, hardening agents, smoothing agents—available at crafts stores.

1. Dipping Candles

Place paraffin in the bottom of a metal ice cube tray and rest it over a pot of boiling water. Adjust the heat so that the wax in the ice cube tray is melted but just at the point of hardening. Holding the ends of the wick in either hand, dip it into the wax. As you raise the wick out, the wax will harden around it. With repeated dippings, additional layers will build up. Continue until it reaches the size taper you want. (An alternative is to solder two coffee cans together, fill with wax, and dip the wicks vertically.)

2. Dipping Havdalah Candles

Follow the above procedure for dipping—but only build up relatively thin, long tapers. Do this for three (or as many tapers as you want in your candle). If you do this quickly enough, or if a few people are working on the separate tapers at the same time, or if you have a few pots going, the tapers will still be soft enough to mold, braid, or twist. If one or two have hardened before the others were ready, simply heat the hardened ones for a bit over the boiler and then braid them together.

Make your first candle with a simple three-braid. Put embellishments on later ones. Remember, the havdalah candle does not have to be made in any one way. It just must have more than one wick and resemble a torch somewhat. An embellishment: after braiding or twisting, dip the whole candle into the melted wax to glaze it and give it a soft, textured effect.

3. For Honeycomb Beeswax Candles

This wax comes in thin rectangular sheets (approximately 8 inches by 12 inches) pressed to the texture of a honeycomb. It is very easy to work with, safe, requires no melting, and is tremendously versatile. The sheets come in a wide range of colors.

To work with it, cut with scissors or knife to the length you want. Place a length of wick along one edge. Beginning with that edge, fold the wax tightly around the wick and roll tightly. Press the other edge lightly so that it adheres to the rest of the candle. Cut off the wick on the bottom. Trim the wick at the top. There is a basic candle.

An elegant variation: instead of using a rectangle, begin with a triangular piece of wax. Place the wick along one edge. When you finish rolling, the candle will have a spiral, tapered appearance.

Practice with the wax to gain an idea of how much wax is needed for what size and thickness.

Be imaginative. Explore the possibilities of this medium. Fortunately, this process can be adapted for making a number of ceremonial candles.

Since you can make these candles virtually any thickness or size, you can easily gauge them to the size of your Hanukkah menorah. Also, these candles are perfect for homemade menorot—particularly those made from wood you have gleaned from forests. Red, yellow, and orange emphasize the flame motif.

Use white sheets rolled into simple candles—tapers for Shabbat or yom tov.

Even havdalah candles can be made from honeycomb wax, but you must do it carefully. Use the entire length of the sheet, but only roll a thin taper. Roll three tapers. Carefully braid the three together.

Wind Wicking around a pencil. Place wax in a can and melt in a pan of water. When wax is liquid, dip wick into wax. Cool in cold water between dips.

63

The wax is bound to crack a bit in the process. This can be patched up. If you hold the tapers over a hot stove while braiding them, you will increase their flexibility. For a final touch, if you happen to have some melted wax around, dip the final braided candle into the wax so as to give it a glaze and seal any cracks which may have occurred while rolling. Also, the effect of the glaze over the honeycomb wax is wonderful.

4. For Oil Candles

These are probably the oldest and simplest type of candles. Fill a small (unbreakable) vessel with olive oil, stick a wick in it, light the wick.

Many Hanukkah menorot from Israel are made of glass with oil cups instead of candle holders. Rather than let these serve simply as ornaments in your house, try using them the way they were originally intended.

ANCIENT OIL LAMP

The Tabernacle in the Wilderness

The Tabernacle model may be used as table centerpiece.

Supplies Needed

> shoe box
> gold-foil paper
> small spice box
> scissors or x-acto knife
> ruler
> pencil
> silk scarves or fabric in colors of red, violet, and
>   blue

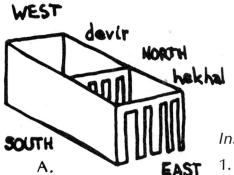

A.

Instructions

1. Cut a section from the box cover the same size as the end of the shoe box.
2. Cut pillar forms out of one end of the box and the cut piece made in step 1 (see illustration A). The cut end of the box becomes the entrance to the tabernacle.
3. Insert cut piece into box to divide the box into two rooms. The room from the insert to the west wall should be square. The insert becomes the entrance to the Holy of Holies (devir).
4. Cover a small spice box with gold-foil paper and place in the devir. This represents the ark of the covenant, which holds the tables of the decalogue. The ark is to face east and has, placed in front of it, a pot of manna and Aaron's rod.
5. The outer chamber is known as the holy place (hekhal). At the north wall was placed the "table of the presence," on which were placed plates of bread, cups for incense, and vessels for wine or oil. At the south wall was placed the menorah of seven lights. The children could draw and color the north-wall furniture and the south-wall menorah and glue them to the respective walls of the model.
6. Drape the silk scarves or fabric over the top of the model from the east wall to the west wall and down to the ground (see illustration B).

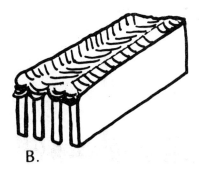

B.

Mizrah

It was customary for Jews to hang an ornament of some kind on the eastern wall of the dining room, as one was to face Jerusalem when praying. This ornament was known as a mizrah, from the Hebrew word meaning "east." Among some Jews in Eastern Europe, elaborate designs were cut from folded paper with a scissors or knife blade, taking full advantage of the symmetry available from this type of work. We are suggesting some mizrah patterns that you and your children may be able to use. Some design elements that were used in the Temple, and are common in Jewish art, are the lion (sign of Judah), the grape, grapevine, and pomegranate (symbols of plenty and God's promises to Israel); bells; shofar (symbols of the Temple service itself); the palm tree with seven branches (tree of life); and the menorah, or Temple candelabra.

MIZRAH

TOP

Instructions

1. Fold an 8½ inch by 11 inch piece of paper into quarters. Carefully trace the design on page 72 using carbon paper.*
2. Cut out the design, except the menorah, with an x-acto knife. Care should be used to keep the four rectangles in line.
3. Unfold the paper to ½ and cut out the menorah.
4. Carefully open the paper to full size, add the Hebrew letters for "mizrah," and cut out.
5. The cut-out design can be mounted on a piece of contrasting paper and hung on an east wall, or it can be hung unmounted in an east window.

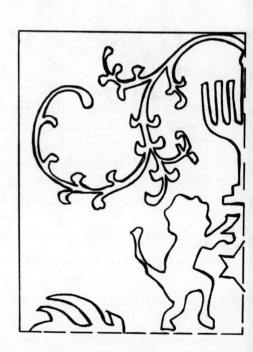

*Be sure you leave a ⅛ inch border between the design and the sides of the paper.

66

Games for Your Havdalah Party

These are adapted from old favorites.

1. For the youngest: Hide the Spice Box; or, Hide the Candle

Before the ceremony, the youngest may hide the spice box or the havdalah candle somewhere in the living room. The adults must find it in order to perform the ceremony. Children may say "you're warm" or "you're cold" to hint at the hiding place, or they may sing a song (what Jewish song did they learn in nursery school—Shalom Aleichem or David Melech Yisrael?), singing loudly when the adult approaches the hiding place and softer when he is far from it.

2. For the Very Youngest: Hide the Candy

Parents may hide *wrapped* candy for children to find after the havdalah ceremony, either giving hints or not as is felt appropriate.

3. My Aunt Abigail Took a Trip to Israel

This is a verbal memory game that will be fun for everyone over four or five years of age. The first player starts, "My Aunt Abigail took a trip to Israel and she packed . . . [fill in any item, such as goggles to go snorkeling at Eilat, or a prayerbook to go to services in Jerusalem]." Each player must correctly repeat all the previous items and then add a new one. When players are unable to do this they are "out," and the last one able to repeat the longest list is the winner. Try to have items related to Israel but "anything goes" on this trip.

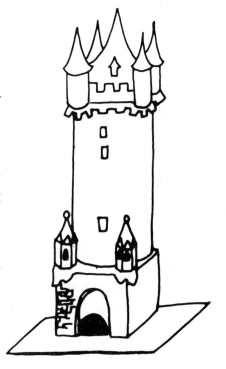

4. Treasure Hunt

Older children can make a treasure hunt with notes and clues to find the havdalah articles or candy.

5. What's Missing?

Assemble on a table, perhaps after dinner Friday night, all symbols of the holiday, and make sure that the children can name them all. Include havdalah symbols. Send one child from the room, remove one object, call him back, and see if he can remember what is missing. Repeat for the other children.

6. Nineteen Questions

A verbal game adaptable for school-age children and older. Based on "twenty questions," this is nineteen because the first question, "Is the person Jewish?" is already answered yes. To remind you, the person who is "it" chooses a famous Jewish personality, and the rest must ask questions to identify him. The questions must be answerable with a yes or a no. For example, "woman?" "living?" "American?" etc. A teenager stumped her family with Marc Chagall, even though they had discovered they were trying to find a living French male Jew.

7. Bible Charades

Divide into two teams with all ages on both teams. Each team writes out Bible quotations for the others to act out. A team member draws a slip and acts out the quote for his team members in pantomime, scoring according to how long it takes to guess the quotation. Better supply each team with a Bible!

8. Jewish Encyclopedia

A paper and pencil game for adults and teenagers. You need a Jewish encyclopedia for this one. The person who is "it" looks up a name, place, or term which all players must agree they cannot define or recognize.

"It" copies a summary of the encyclopedia entry, while each of the other players makes up a fictitious entry, sounding as authentic and correct as possible.

All entries are tossed into a box, and "it" reads them aloud, including the correct one, and everyone votes as to which is the correct answer. Some of the guesses can be hilarious. At the end, "it" reveals the correct answer. The person whose entry gets the most votes is the winner, however.

TRY THIS TONGUE TWISTER!

IN SIX SHARPS SHE SINGS SHABBAT SHALOM

Suggested Activities for Very Young Children

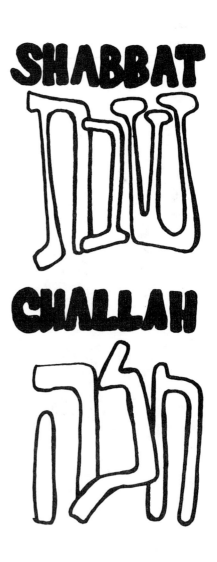

Children should be involved with actual preparation for the holiday—they learn by doing and by playing. If supervised, they can chop vegetables for soup, polish silver, set the table, help with braiding the challah. This is more meaningful than special childish activities just for them. They also learn Hebrew blessings easily "at ages three to six" or "at nursery school age" even if they don't understand the words. Let them light small candles, have their own kiddush cup, and do what their parents do at the Shabbat table. They like repetition.

Children can make table decorations for Shabbat—the parent must be satisfied and accept what the child is able to make. For example:

• Candlesticks—a child can paint spools from your sewing box for little candleholders. He can make candleholders of clay, or even from a styrofoam cup (hot cup) turned upside-down, with a hole in it and covered with aluminum foil.

• Kiddush cup—a child can cover a paper cup with aluminum foil. In our house, the children used to use their silver baby cups for kiddush cups (with grape juice in them).

• Yarmelkes—can be made of construction paper. Cut in a circle and cut out a triangular piece like a slice of pie. Let the child draw on a design or his name with crayon. Tape the two cut sides together to make a cone or cap-shape. Children can make these for the whole family.

• Challah cover—get some loosely woven fabric and let the children ravel the edges to make fringes. If you cut the Hebrew or English letters for "Shabbat" or "challah" out of a piece of cardboard for a stencil, the child can then spatter-paint the design. This is done by dipping an old toothbrush in watercolor and rubbing it on a screen or comb to make drops of paint. (Spread newspapers—this can be messy!) Another way to decorate the fabric is by crayon rubbing. Put the stencil or cutout under the fabric and have the child make many strokes across it—the design will show up.

69

• Napkin rings can be cut from paper tubes, such as paper-towel tubes, and decorated.
• Centerpieces. Flowers can be cut from the cup part of an egg carton, colored, and stems made of pipecleaners or twist-ems. Flowers can also be made of colored tissue gathered together with a pipe-cleaner or twist-em for a stem. Stick the flowers into clay in a vase or jar. In fall dried weeds can be gathered; fresh flowers in spring and summer.
• White paper napkins often have embossed designs that can be colored in with crayons. Paper doilies, too, can be colored.

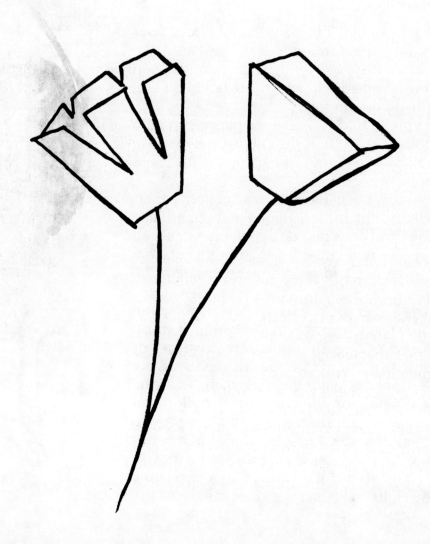

A Saturday Afternoon Nature Walk

Most Jewish thinkers today accept the theory of evolution and the concepts by which archaeology and geology have continually thrust the origins of man into a more remote past. Science enriches our knowledge of the world in which we live, and through it we understand the fascinating complexities of the relationship not only of man and beast (as hinted at in the story of Noah's ark), but of atmosphere, plants, insects, and animals.

Now that we have walked on the uninhabited moon, we should be able to appreciate the life-sustaining properties of the earth more than any preceding generation. Although we are sophisticated enough to know there is no proof of God's existence, we are also sophisticated enough to realize that science will continue to develop new theories and concepts about the universe and its origins.

If we adults can accept the belief that this universe, life, and human consciousness were created by a divine being, then we can find a source for wonder, for appreciation, and for purpose in our lives. If we accept, as the rabbis teach, that man is a partner with God in the continuous work of creation, then we can feel that our lives can be important and meaningful.

A Saturday afternoon nature walk is a good way to think about the marvelous variety and unexplained mysteries of creation—for example, in the autumn, one notes that the leaves are changing color and birds are migrating. You can go to a park where naturalists conduct these walks or you can wander around your own neighborhood—pick up a leaf and look at the elaborate veining in it—pick up another from the same tree and see how different it is and how complex its patterns are. Do you know how this tree fits into the life-patterns of plants, animals, and men?

71

use satin and outline stitches

4
Songs

Blessing for Wine: Kiddush

Ba- ruch a -ta A- do- nai, E- lo- he - nu me- lech ha-o- lam, bo -

rey___ pri___ ha-ga - fen. A - men.

Blessing for Bread: HaMotsi

Ba- ruch a -ta A- do- nai, E- lo- he- nu me- lech ha- o- lam, ha-mo -

tsi___ le- chem min ha - a - rets. A - men.

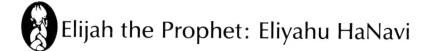

Elijah the Prophet: Eliyahu HaNavi

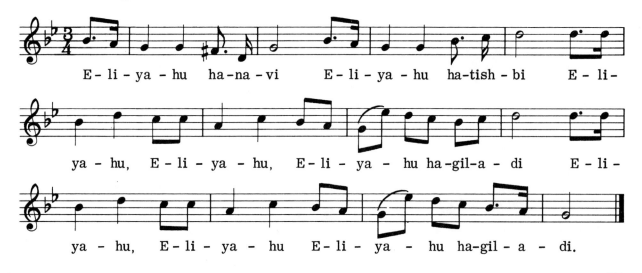

E- li - ya - hu ha- na - vi E- li - ya - hu ha- tish - bi E - li -

ya - hu, E- li - ya - hu, E- li - ya - hu ha- gil- a - di E - li -

ya - hu, E- li - ya - hu E- li - ya - hu ha- gil- a - di.

Blessing the Candles

Ba - ruch a - ta A-do - nai, E - lo - he - nu me - lech ha - o -

lam, A - sher kid-sha-nu b'-mits-va-a - tav, vi - tsi -

va - nu l'-had-lik ner shel_____ Shab - bat.

A Good Week: Shavua Tov

Sha - vu - a tov, sha - vu - a tov, sha - vu - a tov, sha - vu - a

tov, sha - vu - a tov, sha - vu - a tov sha - vu - a tov sha - vu - a tov.

Peace Be With You: Shalom Aleichem

Sha - lom a - lei - chem mal - a - chei_ ha - sha - ret mal - a - chei_ el - yon._____ Mi_____ me - lech mal - a - chei_ ham - la - chim ha - ka - dosh ba - ruch hu.

Bo - a - chem l' - sha - lom mal - a - chei ha - sha - lom mal - a - chei_ el - yon. Mi_ me - lech mal - chei_ ha - m - la - chim ha - ka - dosh ba - ruch_ hu.

Ba - r' - chu - ni l' - sha - lom mal - a - chei ha - sha - lom mal - a - chei_ el - yon. Mi_____ me - lech mal - chei_ ham - la - chim ha - ka - dosh ba - ruch_ hu.

Tset - chem l' - sha - lom mal - a - chei_ ha - sha - lom mal - a - chei_ el - yon._ Mi_____ me - lech mal - a - chei_ ham - la - chim ha - ka - dosh ba - ruch hu.

77

Blessing After Meals: Birkat HaMazon

più mosso

Ka - ka - tuv v'- a - chal - ta v'- sav - a - ta u - vay - rach - ta

et A - do - nai E - lo - he - cha al ha - a - retz ha - to - va a -

sher na - tan lach. Ba - ruch a - ta A - do - nai, al ha -

a - retz v'- al ha - ma - zon. U - v'- ney Ye - ru - sha - la - yim ir ha -

ko - desh bim - hey - ra v'- ya - mey - nu. Ba - ruch a - ta A - do -

nai, bo - nay v'- ra - cha - mav Ye - ru - sha - la - yim A - men.

Judea Forever

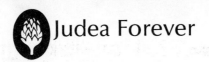

This lovely round means "Judea will live forever, and Jerusalem from generation to generation."

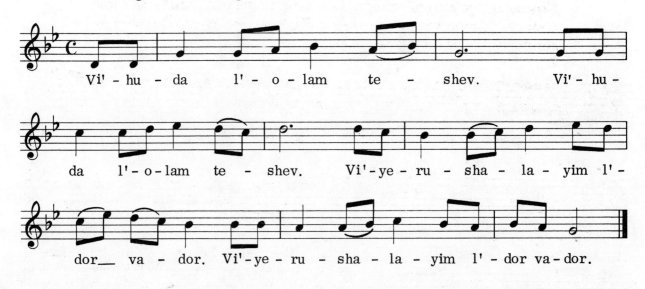

Vi'-hu-da l'-o-lam te-shev. Vi'-hu-da l'-o-lam te-shev. Vi'-ye-ru-sha-la-yim l'-dor__ va-dor. Vi'-ye-ru-sha-la-yim l'-dor va-dor.

To My Land

by Rachel

I sang no song to you No glo-ry gave your name, I
O Moth-er land of mine I know it's ver-y dull, the

did no no-ble deed nor fought in man-y wars. I
gift your daugh-ter brings is ver-y plain in-deed. Is

on-ly plant a tree by peace-ful Jor-dan stream. I
but the sound of joy when morn-ing light will shine, is

on-ly made a path my feet up-on your fields.
on-ly hid-den tears when think-ing of your poor.

 Hevenu Shalom Aleichem

"*Hevenu Shalom Aleichem*" is a song of greeting and welcome.
Two of the meanings of the word *shalom*—"hello" and "peace"—
lend extra warmth to the song.

He - ve - nu sha - lom a - lei - chem,— He - ve - nu
sha - lom a - lei - chem,— He - ve - nu sha - lom a -
lei - chem,— He - ve - nu sha - lom, sha - lom, sha - lom a - lei - chem.

 Shalom Chaverim

"*Shalom Chaverim*" uses the third meaning of the word *shalom*—
"good-bye," as well as "peace." It is a song of departing, saying
farewell. *L'hitraot* means essentially "until we meet again."

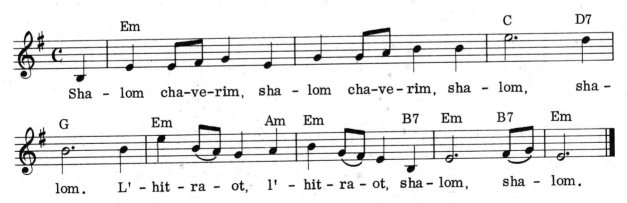

Sha - lom cha-ve-rim, sha - lom cha-ve-rim, sha - lom, sha -
lom. L' - hit - ra - ot, l' - hit - ra - ot, sha - lom, sha - lom.

Hine Ma Tov

"How good it is and how pleasant when brothers sit together"
"Hine Ma Tov" is a nice song for groups to sing, and is an easy
round.

Hi-ne ma tov u-ma-na-im, she-vet a-chim gam ya-chad.

Hi-ne ma___ tov, she-vet a-chim gam ya-chad.

Shabbat Shalom

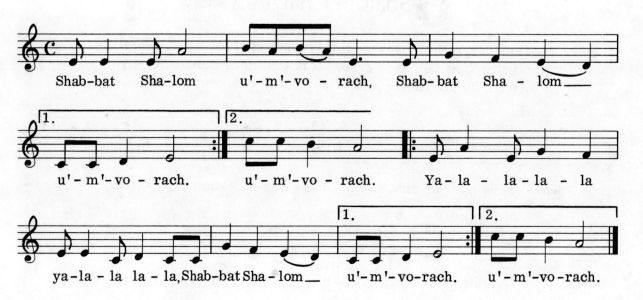

Shab-bat Sha-lom u'-m'-vo-rach, Shab-bat Sha-lom___

u'-m'-vo-rach. u'-m'-vo-rach. Ya-la-la-la-la

ya-la-la la-la, Shab-bat Sha-lom___ u'-m'-vo-rach. u'-m'-vo-rach.

5
Recipes

Recipes for Shabbat

There are many good Jewish cookbooks on the market, and most cooks know how to prepare the traditional Ashkenazi Sabbath meal. Gefilte fish can be bought at markets already prepared, so we have not included a recipe. The usual menu would be chicken soup or gefilte fish, roast chicken or brisket, potatoes or kugel, salad, and a favorite family dessert. However, it is more important to pick a menu that is your family's favorite. The people in our group really enjoyed baking their own Sabbath bread (challah), and we have included a recipe for it. We have also included cholent, a traditional dish that stayed hot for Saturday lunch in a very slow oven.

The recipe section includes a number of recipes from Israel, which may be less familiar to most cooks, and may be especially appropriate when you have a Shabbat observance based on an Israeli theme.

We also include a recipe for cookies for havdalah—the children love to make these—they roll them like clay dough—and they were popular with our families.

SHALOM

A Rabbi once said the Challah was covered so it wouldn't be embarrassed when the wine was the first to be blessed.

Another Rabbi commented: if we are not to embarrass a loaf of bread, how much more must we be careful never to embarrass a human being.

About Challah

Challah is white egg bread, usually braided and sprinkled with poppyseeds or sesame seeds. It is traditional to have two loaves on Friday night. Why two? To recall the double portion of manna sent to our forefathers in the wilderness on Friday so they would not have to do the work of gathering food on the Shabbat.

It is also traditional to cover the challah with an embroidered cloth, and we have included a pattern for such a cloth (see page 61). Many families break the bread, rather than cut it with a knife. That is because the knife is a symbol of warfare and of violence, and the Sabbath table must always be peaceful.

Bread is a symbol of God's sustaining love for mankind. Living in a period of world grain shortages should make us understand that in the past, and even now, bread is more than a symbol for many people. It can be the literal difference between life and death.

The baker traditionally breaks off a bit of the dough and throws it in the fire (or burns it with a match). This is to recall the sacrifices made in the Temple and to remind us of the imperfections of our lives. A piece can also be broken off the loaf after it is baked.

In one lovely home we once visited on a Friday night (that of David and Martha Birnbaum of St. Paul), the father broke a piece of challah and passed it to each child. As he did so, he said something special and thoughtful, commending the youngster on some good thing he had done in the past week, some mitzva the child had performed. Then, when the pieces were all in hand, everyone recited the motzi together.

How to Do It

You can buy your loaves of challah. Get them fresh and unsliced!

You can buy frozen prepared dough for one loaf (made with vegetable oil) and follow the directions on the package. When it says to "shape the dough," divide it in three parts, roll them into sausage shapes, and then braid them. Beat an egg, and brush what is needed on top of the loaf, and sprinkle it with poppyseeds or sesame seeds. Bake according to directions.

If you prefer to go the whole way, here is a recipe, slightly modified, from *The Jewish Catalogue* (reprinted with the permission of the Jewish Publication Society). If you haven't baked bread before, it may be best to ask an experienced baker to help you the first time—or go visit her in her kitchen and watch!

½ cup oil
1 tablespoon salt
1 tablespoon sugar
1½ cups warm water
⅓ cup warm water (105°–115°)
2 packages dry yeast
3 eggs
7 to 7½ cups flour (all-purpose or unbleached)
sesame or poppy seeds

Dissolve the yeast in ⅓ cup warm water and let rest 5 minutes. While doing this, pour the oil, salt, and sugar into a large mixing bowl. Add 1½ cups warm water and stir. Beat 3 eggs. Save 1 tablespoon beaten egg to be brushed on completed loaves, and add the rest to the oil and water mixture. Add dissolved yeast. Stir—add half the flour and stir with a spoon. Gradually add the rest of the flour, working with your hands when it gets thick, up to 7 cups. Turn out on floured board and knead until dough no longer sticks to board or hands—add more flour if necessary. Return dough to bowl and cover with a clean towel. Let rise in a warm place for 1 hour (a gas oven with pilot light is warm enough, or put a bowl of hot water in the oven, and put the bowl of dough with it). It should double in bulk. If poked with your finger, the hole will remain. Turn dough out on lightly floured board and knead 1 minute. Cut into 12 equal pieces and knead each piece until it is not sticky, adding flour if needed. Let rest while you grease a cookie sheet with vegetable shortening. Roll each piece of dough into a strand 8 inches long and then make four braided loaves. Place on baking sheet and let rise for 45 minutes at room temperature. Brush tops of loaves with beaten egg and sprinkle with sesame or poppy seeds. Bake in 375° oven for 40–45 minutes. Remove loaves to racks to cool. Extra loaves may be frozen. For richer flavor, you may want to try more sugar and melted vegetable margarine instead of vegetable oil.

Any good baker will tell you the Challah is covered to keep it warm and with a special cover to make the Sabbath table beautiful.

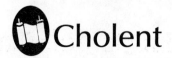Cholent

Cholent is a traditional Shabbat dish, to be eaten on Saturday. Since the Orthodox Jewish housewife does not make a fire or turn on electricity on the Shabbat, this is a way to prepare a hot dish for Saturday lunch. There are many different recipes, but this is a favorite with us.

    4 pounds beef brisket or shortribs
    2 cups dried lima beans, soaked overnight
    salt, pepper, ginger, paprika—to taste
    3 large onions, chopped
    2 tablespoons flour
    2 tablespoons fat or oil

Brown the onions and meat in the bottom of a Dutch oven; season with salt, pepper, paprika, ginger. Drain lima beans, and add to the pot (you may also add barley or potatoes if you wish). Sprinkle with flour. Add boiling water to cover the entire dish. Place tight cover on Dutch oven and put in oven at 250° for 24 hours.

Havdalah Candle Cookies

    1 cup shortening (half butter or margarine, half
      Spry or Crisco)
    1 cup sifted powdered sugar
    1 egg
    1½ teaspoons almond extract
    1 teaspoon vanilla
    2½ cups flour
    1 teaspoon salt

Mix first five ingredients, then sift and stir in the flour and salt. Divide the dough in half, and add a few drops of blue vegetable coloring to half. This dough can be rolled in strips, like clay. Have the children roll out thin strips and braid the blue and white strands to look like havdalah candles.

Bake in ungreased cookie sheet at 375° for about 10 minutes (depending on how thick the braids are). Sprinkle with sugar after baking.

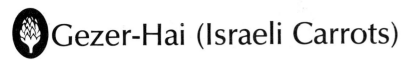 Gezer-Hai (Israeli Carrots)

1 pound firm, fresh carrots
juice of 3 oranges
juice of ½ lemon
dash of ginger (optional)
salt and sugar to taste

Peel the carrots and grate coarsely. Cover with the orange and lemon juice, adding sugar and salt to taste. Add a dash of ginger if desired. Refrigerate for several hours (this salad improves with keeping up to three days) so that the carrots absorb the juices. Serve on crisp lettuce leaves or in lemon baskets garnished with a sprig of mint. (Serves 4–6)

—Allan Hersh

The following five recipes are from the *Israeli Cook Book* by Molly Lyons Bar-David (New York: Crown Publishing Co., 1964, used with copyright permission).

 Schorbach (Tunisian Mint Soup)

1 clove garlic, crushed
½ cup fresh mint leaves or 2 tablespoons dried mint
1 tablespoon cornstarch
1 tablespoon olive oil
4 cups chicken soup
½ cup cold water
3 egg yolks
salt and pepper

Fry the garlic and mint in the oil at low heat 8–10 minutes. Put through a sieve. Add the cornstarch dissolved in cold water and season. Bring chicken soup to a boil, stir in the mint mix, and cook for 5 minutes. Beat egg yolks and slowly add some of the soup, stirring well. Add this to the soup and serve at once.

 # Tehina

1 cup tehina (sesame paste)
2 cloves crushed garlic
3 tablespoons olive oil
1 teaspoon salt
juice of 2 lemons
2 tablespoons chopped parsley

Mix the above and add ½ cup water or more to consistency of mayonnaise.

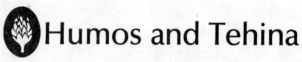 # Humos and Tehina

3 cups chick peas
clove garlic
1 cup tehina (sesame paste) prepared according
   to directions on container
1 tablespoon chopped parsley
1 tablespoon olive oil
juice of 1 large lemon
dash pepper
salt to taste
olives to garnish

Put the chick peas and the other ingredients in a blender, then add the tehina and blend again. Garnish with olives and parsley. This makes a dip for pita (flat bread, which can be purchased in many specialty stores in the United States) or for crackers.

Sesame Fried Chicken

1 cup sesame seed
1 cup flour
2 teaspoons salt
1 egg, beaten
1 frying chicken, in parts
1 paper bag

Mix sesame seed with flour and salt in the paper bag. Dip fryer parts in beaten egg, then shake in the paper bag and fry.

Falafel

½ pound chick peas
3 tablespoons burghul (cracked or bulgar wheat)
2 cloves garlic
1 teaspoon salt
2 tablespoons flour
1 teaspoon cumin
dash of chili pepper
dash of coriander

Soak chick peas overnight, grind them through a meat chopper. Soak burghul 1 hour, then grind it. Mix together with all the rest. Form into small balls and fry in very hot deep fat until golden brown. May be reheated in the oven. (Telma, an Israeli company, makes a very good Falafel mix which is marketed in some stores in the United States.)

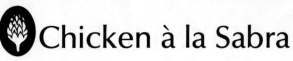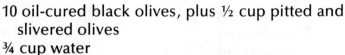

Chicken à la Sabra

10 oil-cured black olives, plus ½ cup pitted and
   slivered olives
¾ cup water
2 3-pound broilers
flour, salt, pepper for coating
1 cup margarine or shortening
2 cups orange juice
1 cup dry red wine
2 large red onions, sliced
2 teaspoons salt
¼ teaspoon black pepper
1½ teaspoons powdered thyme (or less)

Simmer the whole olives in the water for 10 minutes.
Strain. Have the chicken cut into quarters. Coat the
chicken pieces with a mixture of flour, salt, pepper,
and paprika. Melt the margarine in the skillet; add
the chicken and brown lightly. Remove the chicken
from the skillet and place in a large flat casserole. To
the skillet add the orange juice, wine, olive liquor,
onions, salt, pepper, and thyme. Simmer 3 minutes.
Pour the sauce over the chicken and bake 1 hour in a
350° oven, basting occasionally with the sauce.
Spread the ½ cup pitted, slivered olives over the
chicken. Continue baking the chicken 30 minutes
more, or until tender. May be garnished with
mandarin oranges. (Serves 6–8)

—Allan Hersh

 Eggplant Salad

2 medium eggplants
1 small onion
½ cup premixed tehina
1 tablespoon lemon juice
2 cloves garlic
1 teaspoon salt
pepper optional

Bake eggplants in 375° oven until soft; approximately 1 hour. Allow to cool, remove peel, and drain liquid. Chop pulp in food grinder or blender. Grate or chop onion and add to eggplant. Add tehina, lemon juice, crushed garlic, and salt, and mix well. Place in refrigerator. Serve cold on a lettuce leaf, accompanied by pita and Israeli salad.

—Tammy Shachar

6

Readings and Dialogues for Adults

A Sabbath Evening Reading for Adults: Creation

From the Torah

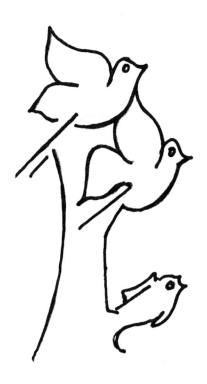

In the beginning, God created the heaven and the earth. Now the earth was unformed and void and darkness was upon the face of the deep; and the spirit of God hovered over the face of the waters.

And God said, "Let there be light," and there was light.

And God saw the light that it was good, and God divided the light from the darkness.

And God called the light Day and the darkness He called Night, and there was evening and morning, one day. . . .

And God said, "Let the waters under the heaven be gathered together unto one place, and let the dry land appear." And it was so . . .

And God said, "Let the earth put forth grass, herb yielding seed, and fruit trees bearing fruit after its kind, wherein is the seed thereof upon the earth." And it was so.

And God said, "Let there be lights in the heavens to divide the day from the night, and let them be for signs and for seasons, and for days and years . . ."

And God saw everything that He had made, and behold, it was very good.

Then God said, "Let us make man in our image, after our likeness; and let them have dominion over the fish of the sea and the birds of the air, and the cattle, and over every creeping thing that creeps upon the earth."

Inspire us to create....

So God created man in His own image, in the image of God He created them, male and female He created them. And God blessed them. . . .

And God saw everything that He had made, and behold, it was very good. And there was evening and morning, a sixth day. . . . And on the seventh day, God finished his work and He rested on the seventh day from all the work which He had done.

Interpretation

When the divine word ended chaos and nothingness,
when God rolled away the darkness from the light,
that was the first moment of creation.
When the first man and the first woman opened their
eyes and beheld earth and heaven,
that was a moment of creation as real as the first,

For the sun is not bright without eyes to see,
the waves of the sea cannot crash and roar without
ears to listen,

And unless life marks off the segments,
time is a dimension without measure.

Though we are finite,
God created us both free and conscious,
able to share in His power of creation.

Every moment that we behold anew the work of God,
the jewels of dew on morning grass,
the smile lighting the face of a child,

Every moment that we work for good,
is a moment of creation.

Lord God, renew in us, in every person,
the morning of human awakening:

Let each dawn rise fresh with hope
as it was in the beginning.

Inspire us to create what is good;
quicken our delight in all that You create.

From *Interpretations*
by Ruth F. Brin

A Sabbath Evening Reading for Adults: Noah

From the Torah

And God said unto Noah: "The end of all flesh is come before Me; for the earth is filled with violence through them; and, behold, I will destroy them with the earth.

Make thee an ark of gopher wood; with rooms shalt thou make the ark, and shalt pitch it within and without . . .

And I, behold, I do bring the flood waters upon the earth, to destroy all flesh, wherein is the breath of life, from under heaven; everything that is in the earth shall perish . . .

And of every living thing of all flesh, two of every sort shalt thou bring into the ark, to keep them alive with thee; and they shall be male and female" . . .

And it came to pass after the seven days, that the waters of the flood were upon the earth. And the rain was upon the earth forty days and forty nights . . .

And all flesh perished that moved upon the earth, both fowl, and cattle, and beast, and every swarming thing that swarmeth upon the earth, and every man . . .

And it came to pass at the end of forty days, that Noah opened the window of the ark which he had made. And he sent forth a dove from him, to see if the waters were abated from off the face of the ground . . .

And the dove came in to him at eventide; and lo in her mouth an olive-leaf freshly plucked; so Noah knew that the waters were abated from off the earth . . .

And God blessed Noah and his sons, and said unto them: "Be fruitful, and multiply, and replenish the earth. . . .

And it shall come to pass, when I bring clouds over the earth, and the bow is seen in the cloud, that I will remember My covenant, which is between Me and you and every living creature of all flesh; and the waters shall no more become a flood to destroy all flesh . . ."

.... and the bow is seen in the cloud, that I will remember My covenant, which is between Me and you and every living creature of all flesh; and the waters shall no more become a flood to destroy all flesh...

99

LET US
REMEMBER
THE BOW
THAT SPANS
THE RETREATING
RAIN-CLOUDS

And God said unto Noah: "This is the token of the covenant which I have established between Me and all flesh that is upon the earth."

Interpretation

When the sun rises and the night falls,
when spring follows close on the heels of winter,

Let us remember God's promise
that the rhythms of earth will uphold life forever.

When we sail, like Noah, on uncertain seas,
in a wooden boat no bigger than a toy;

When we fear, like Noah, that the end may come,
if not to all life, then to us,

When we look for small signs of hope,
a green leaf, or the branch of an olive-tree,

Let us remember the bow that spans the retreating
rain-clouds, and the promises God still keeps for us,
that seed-time and harvest shall not cease.

Let us worship and give thanks to Him
for the fruitful earth, our dwelling place,
for His blessings, bright as the rainbow
in the shining sky.

From *Interpretations*
By Ruth F. Brin

A Sabbath Evening Reading for Adults: Jacob Becomes Israel

From the Torah

And Jacob said, "O God of my father Abraham, and God of my father Isaac, O Lord who saidst unto me 'Return unto thy country and to thy kindred, and I will do thee good.'

"I am not worthy of all the mercies and of all the truth which Thou hast shown to Thy servant . . .

"Deliver me, I pray thee, from the hand of Esau; for I fear him . . . "

And he lodged there that night and took of the cattle which he had with him for a present for Esau, his brother, . . . and he delivered the presents unto the hand of his servants . . . to appease Esau . . .

And he rose up that night, and took his two wives and his two handmaidens and his eleven children, and he took them and sent them over the stream (at the ford of Jabbok).

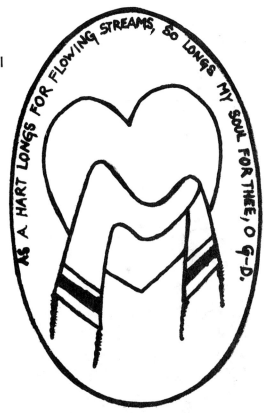

And Jacob was left alone. And a man wrestled with him until the breaking of the day.

And when he saw that he prevailed not against him, he touched the hollow of his thigh; and the hollow of Jacob's thigh was strained, as he wrestled with him.

And he said, "Let me go, for the day breaketh"; and he said, "I will not let thee go, except thou bless me."

And he said "What is thy name?" and he said, "Jacob."

And he said, "Thy name shall be called no more Jacob, but Israel, for thou hast striven with God and with men, and hast prevailed." . . .

And (later) Jacob lifted up his eyes, and looked, and behold, Esau came, and with him four hundred men . . .

And Jacob (went before his wives and his children), and bowed himself to the ground seven times when he came near unto his brother.

And Esau ran to meet him, and embraced him, and fell on his neck, and kissed him; and they wept.

Interpretation

Who can say whether Jacob wrestled with man or angel, with his own fear and guilt, or with God Himself?

I cannot answer, yet I know there is a spirit waiting in the darkness to wrestle with me, and after I meet him, I shall never be the same.

Who can say how Jacob prevailed, in the darkness by the river, against this fearful antagonist?

I cannot answer, yet I am sure there is a river on my way, and when I cross it, I cannot return again.

Who can say whether Jacob was worthy of the mercies that carried him to the wrestling and the river?

Whatever the worthiness of Jacob, surely I cannot pray for help, except to the God of mercy and truth, the God of Jacob.

It is to Him we pray: let all who wait alone in darkness, knowing their fear and their guilt, be unto Thee as Jacob,

Let them be strong with the strength of Jacob's faith, Let them have Jacob's humility, and his courage,

Let them find, when they cross their rivers, the glad peace that Jacob found.

From *Interpretations*
by Ruth F. Brin

find the glad peace that Jacob found

Eternity Utters a Day

A thought has blown the market place away; there is a song in the wind and joy in the trees.

The Sabbath arrives in the world, scattering a song in the silence of the night: eternity utters a day.

Where are the words that could compete with such might?

Six days a week we live under the tyranny of things of space; on the Sabbath we try to become attuned to the holiness in time.

Six days a week we wrestle with the world, wringing profit from the earth; on the Sabbath we especially care for the seed of eternity planted in the soul.

The world has our hands, but the soul belongs to Someone Else.

Six days a week we seek to dominate the world; on the seventh day we try to dominate the self.

To set apart a day a week, a day on which we would not use the instruments so easily turned into weapons of destruction, a day for being with ourselves, a day on which we stop worshiping the idols of technical civilization, a day on which we use no money, a day of armistice in the economic struggle with our fellow-men and the forces of nature—is there any institution that holds out a greater hope for man's progress than the Sabbath?

by Abraham J. Heschel (adapted)

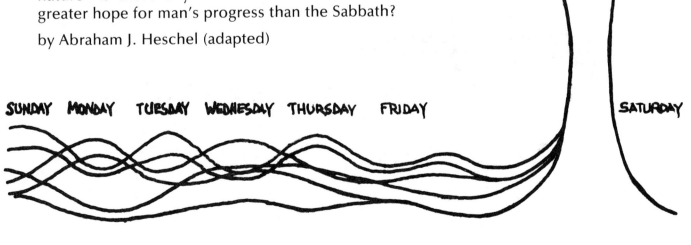

SUNDAY   MONDAY   TUESDAY   WEDNESDAY   THURSDAY   FRIDAY   SATURDAY

Two Poems from Israel

Introduction

During the spring, when Israel celebrates its Independence Day, you may want to read one of these poems by Israeli poets, or sing the song "To My Land," by Rachel, in the music section (p. 80), or let your children dramatize the story of "Hannele" (p. 21), which appears in the second-grade reader used by most Israeli children.

Today there are about 14 million Jews in the world, less than there were in 1940. Today, after the Holocaust, we constitute .04 percent of the population of the world and about 2.8 percent of the population of the United States. Everywhere, except in Israel, we are a tiny minority, speaking many languages and participating in many cultures, and of varying beliefs. Yet we are one people and we live. "Am Yisrael Chai!"—the people of Israel live! We are alive, we are one, and we are unique. In the spirit of joy, we celebrate our brotherhood with our people in Israel and throughout the world at every Shabbat.

AM YISRAEL CHAI AM YIS-
RAEL CHAI AM YISRAEL
CHAI AM YISRAEL CHAI

I Love the Land: A Discovery

by David Eller

David Eller, born in the United States, settled in Israel with his family when he was eight. He was a brilliant student, wrote poetry in English, Hebrew, and Arabic, and "wanted to be the first Israeli ambassador to Cairo." At the age of nineteen he was killed during Israeli army training.

A few nights ago
on my way home
in the darkness of the night,
my beloved country
was revealed to me
in all its beauty.

Out of my joy
I bent and picked
a bunch of green grass
wet from the dew,
cold as the morning,
and I crushed it to my mouth
and kissed the grass,
and kissed its coldness,
and kissed it again. . . .

After I dropped it
in a puddle on my way,
a lonely drop of dew
was left on my lips
as living evidence
of my love.

—Translated by Ruth Brin
with Moti Shachar

Light the Candles

by Zelda

"Zelda" is an Israeli poet, brought up in a traditional way. After raising a large family, she began to write poems in her middle age. They are poignant and lovely works. I believe you would enjoy reading this at your Shabbat table.

Women welcome the Sabbath as a beloved sister: Men welcome her as a radiant Bride.

Light the candles,
Drink the wine.
See how slowly the Sabbath
picks this giant flower,
the setting sun.

See how the Sabbath descends slowly,
and in her hand is the rose of the heavens.

How can she plant
this huge and shining flower
in a blind and narrow heart?

How will the Sabbath plant
this angelic bud
in our mad flesh?
Will the eternal rose
be able to grow
in a generation of slaves,
in a generation of slaves
to destruction and death?

Light the candle,
drink the wine,
The Sabbath descends slowly
and in her hands is the flower,
and in her hands is the setting sun.

—Translated by Ruth Brin
with Moti Shachar

A Day of Rest, Holiness, and Joy

Introduction

Have you ever talked to your children about your religious feelings, concepts, experiences? If you find this difficult, first try it with your husband or wife in the privacy of your bedroom. Or try with a close friend. Or with a rabbi. Do you think we need group sessions to help us "open up" about our religious feelings?

Is religious experience something that will happen to you and me and our children? I think so, not only because I feel that it has happened to me, but because it is known in some form in every human culture. But it is difficult for Western man. A person may try to pray and achieve prayer, but a sense of the divine presence seems to be an experience over which the individual has very little control. A person may feel a change of consciousness, a demand that he carry out a difficult task, a necessity to change his way of life; he may call his experience inspiration, joy, a sense of union with the world or with the divine. He may have a feeling of humility before the vastness and mystery of the universe.

While the religious experience is ultimately ineffable, it has been expressed in dance, prayer, prophecy, leadership of social movements, poetry, music, and art. If we want to achieve it, we need to prepare for it through the ways which are traditional for us: through prayer, singing, Sabbath and holiday observances, the warmth of home and family, participation with other Jews in the life and community of the Jewish people, in synagogue worship, and through study. In those ways, we can be open to such an experience when it comes. We may find a vocabulary through which we can recognize and express such an experience.

A Day of Rest, Holiness, and Joy

Dialogue

FIRST ADULT: Shabbat has been called a "Yom Menuha"—a day of rest, a "Yom Kedusha"—a day of holiness, and a "Yom Taanug"—a day of joy. The Sabbath has been called a bride and a queen, a royal bride. Every one of these seemingly simple phrases has multiple meanings. Each of them begins simply, and grows like an almond tree, with roots reaching into the soul, and beautiful blossoms flowering in the sunshine for all to see.

SECOND ADULT: The day of rest begins with abstaining from work. But the "rest" of Shabbat means tranquility, serenity, harmony, repose, stillness. It means that a person should be at peace with himself, in harmony with family, friends, and community. Can you do that in one day? The Sabbath prescribes prayer, song, thoughtfulness, consideration, celebration. Perhaps not in one day, but perhaps by trying one day a week, year after year, you can achieve Shabbat rest. The Shabbat laws forbid the making of fire, and this has been interpreted to mean that they prohibit the kindling of anger, your own anger or that of others. If you can quiet your soul and achieve Shabbat rest, you may then hear the still, small voice of God.

FIRST ADULT: The day of holiness begins by setting the day aside from other days, as we set aside the Torah from other books. But turning your back on the secular world, abstaining from work, even saying special prayers at home and at the synagogue, is only the beginning. Spiritual renewal, moral redetermination, evaluation of yourself are the next steps. Ultimately, holiness is the imitation of God, Who is holy. It is becoming more like God, more merciful, more kind, more loving, more just, more righteous, more forgiving, more like the God Whom Moses experienced on Mount Sinai. Holiness in Judaism inevitably has moral as well as spiritual connotations, inevitably involves justice as well as mercy, deeds of loving kindness as well as contemplation of God.

SECOND ADULT: The day of joy begins with a sense of celebration, with good food and beautiful clothing

Harvey Cox says that observing the Sabbath requires an altered form of consciousness, similar to meditation for the Eastern religions.

108

and lovely objects—like the candles in their beautiful candlesticks. But it moves toward wholehearted thanks to God for all the good things of creation. Our joy is physical at first, and then it becomes spiritual elevation, mystic joy. Thus the Jewish people have erected a palace, not in space, but in time, a palace each seventh day where they meet the Shabbat, the royal bride. In this palace, at first, it seems that there has been a separation of the holy from the secular, of work from rest, and of Israel from all the other nations. But by these divisions, in this palace, greater unities take place. Life and death no longer seem torn asunder. Body and soul can be knit together, and when this happens, man and God can approach each other.

FIRST ADULT: The Sabbath day becomes a suspension bridge spanning earth and heaven, a meeting place for man and God. We greet the royal bride according to custom and protocol, because she is a queen, but we love her as a bridegroom loves his bride or as a woman loves her daughter when she is a bride. Our celebration is like a wedding, and the consummation of that celebration is on that rare Shabbat when at last we achieve rest, holiness, and joy in the experience of the loving relationship between God and the human soul.

What Kind of Person Was Moses?

Introduction

Every Sabbath incorporates at least three major themes: (1) God's creation of the world, (2) man's experience of God, and (3) the exodus from Egypt. It was in the wilderness, under the leadership of Moses, that we were forged into a people, brought to Sinai, and given the Torah.

There are two different movements in Jewish history that can be designated by the term *exodus*. One is going out of a land of persecution to the Promised Land; the other is going out of a land of persecution to a Land of Promise. The exodus, under Moses, from Egypt to the Land of Israel, the Promised Land, is the archetype of the first. The exodus from Eastern Europe to the United States during the nineteenth and early twentieth centuries is an example of the second. The United States promised Jews freedom to follow their religion and an opportunity to live decently.

There have been many Lands of Promise in our history. When the Romans destroyed Jerusalem, Egypt, Babylon, and Persia were places of refuge and of high Jewish civilization. When the Crusades swept across Western Europe, and Jews were murdered as infidels, Poland was a Land of Promise as the Polish nobility invited the Jews to come to help them manage their estates. When the Inquisition made life intolerable in Spain, Morocco and Turkey offered homes to the Jews. In many of these cases the Land of Promise in turn became a place of persecution which Jews had to leave.

The ultimate destination was always the Promised Land, the Land of Israel, and this is the astonishment of the twentieth century—although Jews have in fact tried to live there throughout the generations, for the first time in nearly two thousand years, Jews once more have their independence there today.

At any Shabbat table during any part of the year, it is appropriate to discuss not only the exodus from Egypt under the leadership of Moses, but all of the departures and arrivals of Jewish history, including those which brought our families where they are

now. We should be able to identify with the exodus from Egypt because we or other members of our families have also experienced exodus. According to the Midrash, every Jewish soul was present at Sinai, those alive then and every Jew born since and every Jew who will be born in the future. We all escaped from Egypt, we all fled through the waters, we suffered in the desert, and we came to Sinai to hear the word of God.

A Dialogue for Adults or Adults and Teenagers

MOE: I always wondered about Moses. He seems to have so many contradictions in his personality.

JOE: Like what?

MOE: He was a leader but he couldn't speak well. He stuttered or had a speech impediment (Exodus 4:10). He was raised as a prince in Pharaoh's palace (Exodus 2:10), but he decided to become one of the Hebrew slaves. Finally, he seemed to be a very practical person—a military leader (Exodus 17:8), but he also must have been a mystic, very religious and solitary (Exodus 33:18–23).

FLO: Well, he didn't really decide to be a Hebrew slave. He decided to lead the slaves out of Egypt, which is a different matter.

JOE: I don't think he was so practical. In chapter 18 of Exodus, it's his father-in-law, Jethro, who tells him how to organize the tribes. Moses was trying to do everything himself, and Jethro told him how to divide the people into smaller groups, with leaders who could ultimately appeal to Moses if they couldn't settle things among themselves. As a military leader he relied on Joshua, and on some practical religious matters, like the priestly functions, Aaron was in charge.

MOE: You can't deny he was a mystic. He spent all that time on the mountain communing with God, and he constantly had visions. Look at the experience of the burning bush that started the whole thing (Exodus 3).

FLO: Call him a mystic if you want to, I'd just say he was the archetype of the Hebrew prophet. He had encounters with God—you can call that mystical experience—but every time he was spurred on to take some sort of action or make some sort of pronouncement. He didn't dissolve into mystical union with the divine like some Hindu mystic types.

111

MOE: Well, he had a bad temper. He broke the tablets when he saw the golden calf (Exodus 32).

FLO: And to get water he struck the rock instead of speaking to it—because he got so angry at the people. God considered that a major sin, you know (Numbers 20).

JOE: You mean after all this discussion, the only thing you two can agree on is that Moses had a bad temper? No wonder they don't write about him in the Haggadah!

MOE: They don't write about him because they used to fear the Jews would worship him. We'd better start over again. Are you willing to admit he was the first monotheist?

JOE: No, I think Abraham was the first. But Moses may have been the first monotheist to teach a whole people—a whole group of tribes—that there is just one God. Abraham only spoke to his own family.

MOE: And maybe Abraham thought other people had other gods, even if he had only one God.

FLO: I think the whole point is that Moses led the Jews out of Egypt. And God helped him. What if we had stayed in Egypt? We'd all be Egyptians by now, or dead, or assimilated . . . there certainly wouldn't be a Jewish people.

MOE: Well, I agree. And this leader wasn't a god or semi-divine person of some sort—he was a real man, with all the complexities and contradictions of a human being. And yet he did a fantastic thing! He created a people that are still alive today. He must be one of the greatest geniuses that ever lived.

7

Sabbath Blessings and Ceremonies

Brief Form of Sabbath Blessings

1. Candles

Baruch ata Adonai, elohenu melech ha-olam, asher kidshanu b'mitzvotov vitzivanu l'hadlik ner shel Shabbat. Blessed art Thou, O Lord our God, Master of the universe, who hast hallowed us by Thy commandments and commanded us to kindle the Sabbath lights.

בָּרוּךְ אַתָּה יְיָ, אֱלֹהֵינוּ מֶלֶךְ הָעוֹלָם, אֲשֶׁר קִדְּשָׁנוּ בְּמִצְוֹתָיו וְצִוָּנוּ לְהַדְלִיק נֵר שֶׁל שַׁבָּת.

2. Kiddush

Baruch ata Adonai, elohenu melech ha-olam, boray p'ri hagofen. Blessed art Thou, O Lord our God, Master of the universe, who createst the fruit of the vine.

בָּרוּךְ אַתָּה יְיָ, אֱלֹהֵינוּ מֶלֶךְ הָעוֹלָם, בּוֹרֵא פְּרִי הַגָּפֶן.

3. Bread

Baruch ata Adonai, elohenu melech ha-olam, ha motzi lechem min ha-aretz. Blessed art Thou O Lord our God, Master of the universe, who bringest forth bread from the earth.

בָּרוּךְ אַתָּה יְיָ, אֱלֹהֵינוּ מֶלֶךְ הָעוֹלָם, הַמּוֹצִיא לֶחֶם מִן הָאָרֶץ.

4. Grace After Meals

Baruch she-achalenu mishelo uvtuvo chayinu. Baruch ata adonai elohenu melech ha-olam, hazan et haolam kulo b'tuvo b'chen b'chesed uvracha-min. We will bless our God of whose bounty we have partaken. Blessed art thou, O Lord our God, Master of the Universe, who sustainest the whole world with they goodness, grace, lovingkindness and mercy.

בָּרוּךְ שֶׁאָכַלְנוּ מִשֶּׁלּוֹ וּבְטוּבוֹ חָיִינוּ.

בָּרוּךְ אַתָּה יְיָ, אֱלֹהֵינוּ מֶלֶךְ הָעוֹלָם, הַזָּן אֶת־הָעוֹלָם כֻּלּוֹ בְּטוּבוֹ. בְּחֵן, בְּחֶסֶד וּבְרַחֲמִים.

Alternate Grace After Meals, From the Traditional Aramaic

Brich rachmana malcha, marah d'hai pitah. Blessed is the All-merciful King, creator of this food.

בְּרִיךְ רַחֲמָנָא מַלְכָּא, מָרָא דְּהַאי פִּתָּא.

Traditional Form of Sabbath Blessings

1. Lighting the Sabbath Candles

The Sabbath candles are lit to formally welcome the Sabbath into the home. It has been traditional for the wife to bless and light the candles, but the entire family may participate in this ceremony.

The candles should be lit approximately twenty minutes before sunset.

Here is the blessing—it should be recited *after* lighting the candles.

בָּרוּךְ אַתָּה יְיָ, אֱלֹהֵינוּ מֶלֶךְ הָעוֹלָם, אֲשֶׁר קִדְּשָׁנוּ בְּמִצְוֹתָיו וְצִוָּנוּ לְהַדְלִיק נֵר שֶׁל שַׁבָּת.

Blessed art Thou, O Lord our God, Master of the universe, who hast hallowed us by Thy commandments and commanded us to kindle the Sabbath lights.

Baruch ata Adonai elohenu melech ha-olam, asher kidshanu b'mitzvotov vitzivanu l'hadlik ner shel Shabbat.

For the music to this blessing, please see the song section, page 76.

2. Kiddush

After everyone has been seated at the Sabbath dinner table, the meal is formally begun with recitation of the kiddush (sanctification) by the head of household holding a cup of wine in his (her) hands.

Baruch ata Adonai, eloheynu melech ha-olam, boray p'ri hagafen. [Amen.] Baruch ata Adonai, eloheynu melech ha-olam, asher kidshanu b'mitsvotav v'ratsa vanu, v'sh'abat kod'sho b'ahavah uvratson hinchilanu, zikaron l'maaseh b'reshit. Ki hu yom t'chilah l'mikraey kodesh, zecher litsiat Mitzrayim. Ki vanu vacharta v'otanu kidashta mikol ha'amim, vshabat kodsh'cha b'ahavah uvratson hinchaltanu. Baruch ata Adonai, m'kadesh hashabat.

[Amen.]

בָּרוּךְ אַתָּה יְיָ, אֱלֹהֵינוּ מֶלֶךְ הָעוֹלָם, בּוֹרֵא פְּרִי הַגָּפֶן. בָּרוּךְ אַתָּה יְיָ, אֱלֹהֵינוּ מֶלֶךְ הָעוֹלָם, אֲשֶׁר קִדְּשָׁנוּ בְּמִצְוֹתָיו וְרָצָה בָנוּ, וְשַׁבַּת קָדְשׁוֹ בְּאַהֲבָה וּבְרָצוֹן הִנְחִילָנוּ, זִכָּרוֹן לְמַעֲשֵׂה בְרֵאשִׁית. כִּי הוּא יוֹם תְּחִלָּה לְמִקְרָאֵי קֹדֶשׁ, זֵכֶר לִיצִיאַת מִצְרָיִם. כִּי בָנוּ בָחַרְתָּ וְאוֹתָנוּ קִדַּשְׁתָּ מִכָּל הָעַמִּים, וְשַׁבַּת קָדְשְׁךָ בְּאַהֲבָה וּבְרָצוֹן הִנְחַלְתָּנוּ. בָּרוּךְ אַתָּה יְיָ, מְקַדֵּשׁ הַשַּׁבָּת.

Blessed art Thou, Lord our God, King of the universe, who creates the fruit of the vine.

Blessed art Thou, Lord our God, King of the universe, who hast sanctified us with thy commandments and hast been pleased with us; in love and favor hast given us thy holy Sabbath as a heritage, a memorial of the creation—that day being also the first among the holy festivals, in remembrance of the exodus from Egypt. Thou hast chosen us and hallowed us above all nations, and in love and favor hast given us thy holy Sabbath as a heritage. Blessed art Thou, O Lord, who hallowest the Sabbath.

3. Blessing When Washing Hands

Following the kiddush, everyone ritually washes his hands for the Sabbath meal by pouring water over the hands and reciting:

Baruch ata adonai, elohenu melech ha-olam, asher kidshanu b'mitzvotav v'tzivanu al netilat yadayim.

בָּרוּךְ אַתָּה יְיָ, אֱלֹהֵינוּ מֶלֶךְ הָעוֹלָם, אֲשֶׁר קִדְּשָׁנוּ בְּמִצְוֹתָיו וְצִוָּנוּ עַל נְטִילַת יָדַיִם.

Blessed art Thou, Lord our God, King of the universe, who has sanctified us with His commandments and commanded us concerning the washing of the hands.

4. Blessing the Bread

Immediately following this, the head of household removes the covering from the challot. Two challot are usually used, symbolic of the two sacrifices offered in the ancient Temple on the Sabbath or the double portion of manna that was gathered by the Israelites on Friday (Exodus 16:22). The challot should be covered with a special decorative Sabbath napkin.

Baruch ata Adonai, elohenu melech ha-olam, ha motzi lechem min ha-aretz. Blessed art Thou O Lord our God, Master of the universe, who bringest forth bread from the earth.

בָּרוּךְ אַתָּה יְיָ, אֱלֹהֵינוּ מֶלֶךְ הָעוֹלָם, הַמּוֹצִיא לֶחֶם מִן הָאָרֶץ.

For the music to this blessing, please see the song section, page 75.

118

Grace After Meals

The grace (birkat ha-mazon) is recited after the meal is completed and the dishes have been removed from the table. It is a tradition which provides the opportunity for singing and celebrating together, as well as thanking God for the food. Following the Hebrew and the transliteration is an interpretation of the "birkat" written by Ruth Brin. Music is on page 78.

LEADER:

    Ra-bo-tai, n'vo-rekh

רַבּוֹתַי נְבָרֵךְ.

RESPONSE:

    Ye-hi shem a'do-noy m'vo-rokh me-a-toh v'ad o-lom

יְהִי שֵׁם יְיָ מְבֹרָךְ מֵעַתָּה וְעַד עוֹלָם.

LEADER:

    Birshut maranan v'rabanan v'rabotai, nevorech she-achalnu mishelo

בִּרְשׁוּת מָרָנָן וְרַבָּנָן וְרַבּוֹתַי,
נְבָרֵךְ שֶׁאָכַלְנוּ מִשֶּׁלּוֹ.

RESPONSE:

    Baruch she-achalnu mishelo uv'tuvo hayenu

בָּרוּךְ שֶׁאָכַלְנוּ מִשֶּׁלּוֹ וּבְטוּבוֹ חָיִינוּ.

IN UNISON:

Ba-ruch a-ta adonoy eloheynu melech ha-olam, hazon et ha-olom kulo b'tu-vo b'chen b'chessed u-v'ra-chamim, hu no-ten le-chem l'chol ba-sar kee l'olam has-do u-v'tu-vo ha-gadol tamid lo chasar la-nu v'al yech-sar la-nu mazon l'-olam va-ed, ba-a'vur sh'mo ha-gadol, ki hu el zon u-m'farnes la-kol, u-may-tiv la-kol, u-may-chin mazon l'chol b'ri-yotav a'sher bara. Ba-ruch a-ta adonoy hazon et ha-kol.

בָּרוּךְ אַתָּה יְיָ אֱלֹהֵינוּ מֶלֶךְ הָעוֹלָם. הַזָּן אֶת־הָעוֹלָם כֻּלּוֹ, בְּטוּבוֹ, בְּחֵן בְּחֶסֶד וּבְרַחֲמִים: הוּא נוֹתֵן לֶחֶם לְכָל־בָּשָׂר, כִּי לְעוֹלָם חַסְדּוֹ: וּבְטוּבוֹ הַגָּדוֹל תָּמִיד לֹא־חָסַר לָנוּ, וְאַל־יֶחְסַר לָנוּ מָזוֹן לְעוֹלָם וָעֶד: בַּעֲבוּר שְׁמוֹ הַגָּדוֹל, כִּי הוּא אֵל זָן וּמְפַרְנֵס לַכֹּל, וּמֵטִיב לַכֹּל, וּמֵכִין מָזוֹן לְכָל־בְּרִיוֹתָיו אֲשֶׁר בָּרָא: בָּרוּךְ אַתָּה יְיָ, הַזָּן אֶת־הַכֹּל:

Ka-katuv v'a-chal-ta v'sa-va-ta u-vay-rach-ta et adonoy e'lo-he-cha al ha-aretz ha-tovah a-sher na-tan loch. Bo-ruch a-ta adonoy, al ha-aretz v'al ha-mazon.

כַּכָּתוּב: וְאָכַלְתָּ וְשָׂבָעְתָּ וּבֵרַכְתָּ אֶת־יְיָ אֱלֹהֶיךָ עַל־הָאָרֶץ הַטֹּבָה אֲשֶׁר־נָתַן לָךְ: בָּרוּךְ אַתָּה יְיָ, עַל הָאָרֶץ וְעַל הַמָּזוֹן:

U-vney y-ru-sha-layim eer ha-kodesh bim-hay-rah v'ya-may-nu. Ba-ruch a-ta adonoy, bo-nay v'ra-ha-mav y-ru-sha-layim. Amen.

וּבְנֵה יְרוּשָׁלַיִם עִיר הַקֹּדֶשׁ, בִּמְהֵרָה בְיָמֵינוּ. בָּרוּךְ אַתָּה יְיָ. בּוֹנֶה בְרַחֲמָיו יְרוּשָׁלָיִם. אָמֵן:

Migdol y'shu-ot malko v'o-seh chesed lim-shicho l'david u-l'zar-o ad o-lam. Oseh shalom bim-romav, hu ya-a'seh shalom o-laynu v'al kol yisrael v'im-ru Amen.

מִגְדּוֹל יְשׁוּעוֹת מַלְכּוֹ, וְעֹשֶׂה חֶסֶד לִמְשִׁיחוֹ, לְדָוִד וּלְזַרְעוֹ עַד עוֹלָם. עֹשֶׂה שָׁלוֹם בִּמְרוֹמָיו, הוּא יַעֲשֶׂה שָׁלוֹם, עָלֵינוּ וְעַל כָּל יִשְׂרָאֵל, וְאִמְרוּ אָמֵן:

An English Interpretation of the Grace After Meals

We praise You, O Lord our God, Master of the Universe,
Who provides food for every living thing.

In the order of nature, you have provided the means of sustenance for man and all Your creatures.

To sustain us, O Lord, You have granted many gifts in Your lovingkindness.

To sustain all mankind, You have granted freedom to follow Your ways.

As we have enjoyed the fruits of the earth and of human labor in eating this food,

So may we enjoy the fruits of our traditions, even as we strive to enhance them.

May the abundance of this meal remind us of the generous gifts of God.

May the fellowship at this table remind us to strive for the brotherhood of man.

We thank You for liberation from bondage and the heritage of Eretz Yisrael.

We thank You for the light of Torah and the guidance of Your commandments

We thank You for the blessing and joy of the Sabbath and holy days.

May gratitude for Your abundant gifts sustain us in the dark hours of sorrow, anxiety, and disappointment

May we live in dignity and honor, free of the yoke of oppression

May this abundant meal which we have eaten together in fellowship remind us of Your gifts and of our goal of brotherhood for all mankind.

Three Traditions to Add to Your Friday Night Celebration

1. Zedakah Box

Make a "zedakah box," and let each member of the family put in a coin. This allows your children to experience the giving of charity, which is often done by you in a pledge or check that they know nothing about.

2. Husband's Praise of His Wife

(Here is a contemporary and abbreviated version of Proverbs 31, the "Ayshet Chayil.")

A good wife, who can find?
She is far more precious than jewels.

The heart of her husband trusts in her,
She does him good all the days of her life.

She rises while it is yet night
and provides food for her household.

She is not afraid of snow for her household
for all her family are clothed in scarlet wool.

She opens her hands to the poor
and reaches out her hands to the needy.

Strength and dignity are her clothing
and she laughs at the time to come.

She opens her mouth with wisdom
and the teaching of kindness is on her tongue.

Her children rise up and call her blessed,
her husband also, and he praises her:

"Many women have done valiantly,
but you surpass them all;
your works are your praise."

3. Traditional Blessing of Children

The father places his hands on the heads of his sons and says, "May God make you like Ephraim and Manasseh." He places his hands on his daughters' heads and says, "May God make you like Sarah, Rebecca, Rachel, and Leah."

To both sons and daughters he says, "The Lord bless you and keep you; the Lord make His face to shine upon you and be gracious unto you; the Lord turn His face to you and give you peace."

Explanation of blessings: Ephraim and Manasseh were the sons of Joseph. They received a special blessing from Jacob [Genesis 48] because they (like Moses) were raised as princes in the court of Egypt, yet they chose to remain Jews. Jewish parents want their sons to show the same loyalty to their God and their people. The girls, it is hoped, will be like the wives of the patriarchs: Sarah was beautiful, Rebecca was intelligent, Rachel was loving and beloved, Leah had many children. Each was a personality who played an important individual role in the history of the Jewish people.

יְשִׂמְךָ אֱלֹהִים כְּאֶפְרַיִם וְכִמְנַשֶּׁה.

יְשִׂמֵךְ אֱלֹהִים כְּשָׂרָה רִבְקָה רָחֵל וְלֵאָה.

יְבָרֶכְךָ יְיָ וְיִשְׁמְרֶךָ:
יָאֵר יְיָ פָּנָיו אֵלֶיךָ וִיחֻנֶּךָּ:
יִשָּׂא יְיָ פָּנָיו אֵלֶיךָ וְיָשֵׂם לְךָ שָׁלוֹם.

4. Alternative suggestion for blessing of children

The blessing of girls from "Fiddler on the Roof" reflects most of the traditional ideas. Perhaps your family can sing part or all of it together:

> May the Lord protect and defend you
> May He always shield you from shame
> May you come to be in Yisrael a shining name.
> May you be like Ruth and like Esther
> May you be deserving of praise.
> Strengthen them, O Lord, and keep them
> from the stranger's ways.
> May God bless you and grant you long lives
> May God make you good mothers and wives
> May he send you husbands who will care for you
> May the Lord protect and defend you
> May the Lord preserve you from pain
> Favor them, O Lord
> With happiness and peace,
> O hear our Sabbath prayer, Amen.

122

The custom of expressing appreciation to the wife and mother and the custom of blessing the children can add moments of sweetness and love to your Shabbat at home. Yet you may realize, as have others, that there is no similar expression of wife to husband or children to parents. In his Shabbat manual, Rabbi Gunther Plaut suggests that children should say, "May God bless our love for one another."

The Wife's Reply

A New Response to the
"Ayshet Chayil"

by Ruth F. Brin

> A good family is a special and wonderful thing—people who trust each other and who care for each other.
> A good family means people who listen to each other,
> Who open their hearts and their minds to one another.
>
> Each member understands that he is an important person
> Each member understands that he has responsibilities to each of the others
> In a good family, some work in the home and some work outside of it,
> but all work together, and everyone works to grow and to learn,
> each in his own way.
>
> A good family is a blessing from God
> to be treasured and enjoyed.
> With thanks in our hearts we pray that we can find the ways
> always to be a good family.

A Good Family is a Blessing from G-d to be Treasured and Enjoyed

The Havdalah Service

1. Introduction to Havdalah

A Saturday afternoon in January, when it gets dark early, is a fine time to introduce havdalah to your family, by having a party for another family with children of the same age. All you need to serve is cookies and a beverage—grape juice or hot cocoa for children, wine and coffee or tea for adults. A special cookie recipe is included on page 88 , and some shops carry cookie-cutters in such shapes as six-pointed stars if you or your children enjoy baking. We have also included games and everything you need to celebrate the closing of the Sabbath. Have a good time!

Havdalah is a lovely ceremony performed at sundown Saturday, the ending of the Sabbath. A simple form of the service is included (see page 126).

The meaning of havdalah is "separation" or "distinction." God is thanked for the gifts of wine, light, and fire, and for making the distinction between the holy and the secular, between light and darkness, between the Sabbath and the working days, and between Israel and the other nations. These distinctions are so suggestive that if you have older children or other adults at your party, you may find food for an important discussion. What is the difference between the holy and the ordinary? Between the Jews and other nations? What separates the mature from the immature? What distinguishes good from evil?

2. What You Will Need for the Havdalah Service

1. Wine in a kiddush cup or regular wine glass. Grape juice for children.
2. A spice box or b'somim. These are usually filled with sweet-smelling spices like cinnamon, allspice, or nutmeg. Through the ages craftsmen have made many beautiful spice boxes in a variety of designs—castles or towers

with flags on top, flowers or trees, even windmills. They have been made of silver or other metals. Such a spice box, if you don't have one, may be purchased from a synagogue gift shop or a Jewish book and gift store, or a friend may send one from Israel. It would make a fine anniversary gift from one spouse to the other. However, if you do not have one, you can improvise one easily.

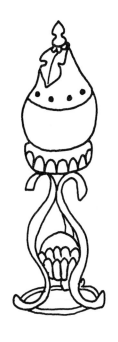

For example, cover a cinnamon box with aluminum foil. Or take a small jar, such as a baby food jar or spice jar, and poke holes in the top so you can smell the spices. You can decorate the jar, or have your children do it, with poster paint, by pasting colored paper or wall paper with a small pattern over it, or by cutting out colored paper and pasting pieces on it. You can also cover the jar with glue and wrap scraps of brightly colored yarn around it in random patterns, letting the yarn stick to the glue. Possibly you can let each child make one for himself.

3. A havdalah candle. You can usually buy the typical blue-and-white braided candle at delicatessens or other Jewish supply stores. You can also improvise simply by holding two Sabbath candles or any other two candles together, or putting them in one large candle-holder, so that there is more than one flame. Or see directions for making candles page 62.

4. A tray or plate and candle-holder for the candle. The reason to keep everything on the tray or plate is that it is customary to fill the winecup to overflowing—for a week overflowing with good things—and then, when the ceremony is over, to quench the flame of the candle in the wine.

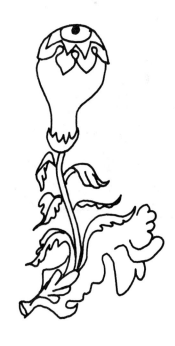

Families in the Chicago Jewish Center made their own candle-holders of quick-drying clay. They let each of their small children make a handprint in a clay plaque and then make an indentation for the candle in the center of the hand. Each child then has his or her individual candle-holder. However, any candlestick you have is acceptable.

3. Directions for the Havdalah Service

The havdalah service consists of blessing the wine, spices, and fire, and the separation God made between the holy and everything else.

Kiddush

בָּרוּךְ אַתָּה יְיָ, אֱלֹהֵינוּ מֶלֶךְ הָעוֹלָם, בּוֹרֵא פְּרִי הַגָּפֶן.

Baruch ata Adonai, Elohenu melecho ha-olam, boray p'ri hagofen. We praise You, O Lord our God, King of the universe, for creating the fruit of the vine. (Hold up the cup while singing.)

B'somim

בָּרוּךְ אַתָּה יְיָ, אֱלֹהֵינוּ מֶלֶךְ הָעוֹלָם, בּוֹרֵא מִינֵי בְשָׂמִים.

Baruch ata Adonai, Elohenu melech ha-olam, boray minay b-somim. We praise You, O Lord our God, King of the universe, for creating various spices. (Inhale the spices and pass the container to everyone there.)

Ha-Aish

בָּרוּךְ אַתָּה יְיָ, אֱלֹהֵינוּ מֶלֶךְ הָעוֹלָם, בּוֹרֵא מְאוֹרֵי הָאֵשׁ.

Baruch ata Adonai, Elohenu melech ha-olam, boray mi-oray ha-aish. We praise You, O Lord our God, King of the universe, for creating the lights of fire. (Cup your hands and extend them toward the havdalah candle, pass the candle around, or allow the youngest child to hold it as high as possible.)

Havdalah

בָּרוּךְ אַתָּה יְיָ, אֱלֹהֵינוּ מֶלֶךְ הָעוֹלָם, הַמַּבְדִּיל בֵּין קֹדֶשׁ לְחֹל.

Baruch ata Adonai, Elohenu melech ha-olam hamavdil ben kodesh l'chol. We praise You, O Lord our God, King of the universe, who has made a distinction between the holy and the ordinary, between light and darkness, between the people of Israel and the other peoples of the world, between the seventh day and the six working days of the week. We praise You, O Lord our God, for distinguishing between the holy and the secular. (Drink the wine. Then a little wine is spilled in a saucer, unless it has already overflowed, since it is customary to fill the cup to overflowing, and the candle is extinguished in the wine. The lights are turned on and everyone wishes everyone else a good week—"Shavua Tov." This song may be sung at this time (see page 76 for words and music). Also, since the Sabbath

126

is now over, it is customary to sing "Eliyahu haNavi"—"Elijah the Prophet." According to Jewish legend, Elijah will come before the Messiah, but the Messiah cannot come on a Sabbath because it would disturb pious observance of the holiday. Therefore, as soon as the holiday is over, a song calling to Elijah to come is sung. One melody for this song is found on page 75.

Afterword

The Jewish tradition has a prayer for almost everything; for morning and evening, for holidays and rites of passage, for hearing thunder, seeing the ocean, tasting the first fruits of the season, smelling fragrant oils or receiving good news. But if there is ever any question as to the appropriate blessing or way to give thanks, Jews can always recite the "She-hechiyanu," a blessing that thanks God for keeping us alive and enabling us to reach this very moment. Now that we have completed this book, we wish to repeat this prayer and hope that you, too, will say it often at times of joy and importance in your lives.

Baruch ata Adonai Elohenu melech ha-olam she-hech-hiyanu v'kiyamanu v'higianu lazman hazeh.

Blessed art, Thou, O Lord our God, master of the universe, who has kept us in life, and has preserved us and enabled us to reach this season.

בָּרוּךְ אַתָּה יְיָ, אֱלֹהֵינוּ מֶלֶךְ הָעוֹלָם, שֶׁהֶחֱיָנוּ וְקִיְּמָנוּ וְהִגִּיעָנוּ לַזְּמַן הַזֶּה.